Great Aussie Jokes

Great Aussie Jokes

Compiled by Sonya Plowman
Illustrated by Geoff Hocking

The Five Mile Press

Contents

Have You Heard the One About...

An elephant, a penguin, and an
Irishman walk into a pub.
'What's going on?' asks the bartender
suspiciously. 'Is this supposed to be a joke?'

★

Some people love reading jokes, some love
telling them. Still others (we'll call them the slightly
thick ones) just like knowing the punchline in
advance so they're not left with a vacant look as
everyone around them guffaws at a joke.
Whether you are on the telling or receiving end
of a joke, this collection will give you enough
material to ensure you'll never again have to

face those embarrassing end-of-joke silences that cause your name to be permanently banished from party invitation lists.

The jokes here run the gauntlet from those you could tell your Gran through to those you wouldn't dare tell your partner. But one thing's for sure: they've all been scientifically tested and there are gut aches to prove it!

The Sick, Dirty and Downright Disgusting chapter should, by its heading alone, warn you not to enter if you're at all easily offended. But if you don't like jokes that are lewd, crude and smutty, you're missing out on the best of them.

So read on...there are blonde jokes aplenty, and male chauvinist pigs have their very own chapter. You'd be wise not to tell any of *those* jokes to your girlfriend – it could mean a black eye or two! Of course, if she's *blonde* she probably wouldn't get them anyway...

Sonya Plowman

Sex, Love and Marriage

Nicki accompanied her husband to the doctor's office. After the check-up the doctor took Nicki aside and said, 'Your husband is suffering from severe long-term stress and it's affecting his health. If you don't do the following four things, your husband will surely die. First, each morning, fix him a tasty breakfast and send him off to work happy. Second, at lunch time, make him a warm, nutritious meal and give him a whole lot of kisses before he goes back to work. Third, after dinner, give him a massage and make sure you don't nag him about anything. Fourth, and most important for relieving stress, have sex with him every day in whatever position he fancies.' On the way home in the car, the husband turned to Nicki and said, 'So, I saw the doctor talking to you and he sure seemed serious. What did he tell you?'

'You're going to die,' she replied.

One day a simple lad visits a brothel and knocks on the door and says to the Madam opening it, 'I want a woman!' The Madam looks at him and says, 'You want a woman, huh? Have you done this before?' the Madam asks, doubtful. 'No.' The Madam laughs and says, 'I'll tell you what, you go and practise with the knotholes in those trees and when you know what you're doing, you come back and see me.' So the lad goes out and finds a knothole. Two weeks later he goes back to the brothel and says to the Madam, 'I want a woman. I know how to do it now!' So the Madam sends him off with one of her girls. When they get to the room the lad tells her to take off her clothes and bend over. When she does he takes out a length of wood and smacks her on the butt. 'What the hell did you do that for!' she exclaims. The lad replies, 'Checking for bees.'

★

Policemen had been working for months on a murder case and had just been given a valuable lead. The suspect was known in the criminal world as Alan Shagbreak. Constable Wagner drove around to the suspect's place of employment and said to the woman at reception, 'Have you got a Shagbreak here?' She scoffed, 'You have got to be joking. The boss here is so stingy we don't even get a tea break.'

★

A woman is in hospital, about to give birth to her first child. She gives a big gasp, and suddenly the baby's head appears. The baby turns to the first man he sees and says, 'Are you my father?' The man replies that he is the doctor, and that the father had not made it to the hospital yet. So the baby says, 'Well, I'm not coming out until my father shows up. Tap three times on my mother's stomach when he turns up and then I'll come out.' With that he returns to his mother's womb. The father turns up an hour later. The doctor duly taps on the mother's stomach three times and down comes the baby. He looks around, sees his father and calls him over. With his little finger he pokes the father in the nose, in the eye, and in the ear. While the father is wincing he says, 'So now you know how it feels. Not very nice is it?'

★

A weary traveller stopped at a hotel in the middle of the night, only to be told that there were no rooms available. 'You've got to have something,' pleaded the traveller. 'Even a spare bed somewhere will do.'

The hotel manager thought for a moment, then said, 'Well, we do have one spare bed, but it's in a room with a really loud snorer. This guy snores so loudly that everyone has been complaining about him. You probably won't get any sleep if you share a room with him.'

'I don't care — I'll take it!' said the traveller with relief. The next morning he went down to breakfast bright-eyed and refreshed. 'So the snorer wasn't a problem for you then?' asked the hotel manager, surprised.

'Nope. As we were going to bed, I bent over him, kissed him and said, "Good night, gorgeous" and he stayed awake all night watching me!'

Sometimes I wake up grumpy; other times I let her sleep.

Thomas and Melanie found it hard to get a babysitter and they decided that the only way to pull off a quickie at home was to send their eight year old son out on the balcony. The boy, pretending to be a super spy, began to report all the neighbourhood activities. 'Mrs Smith is hanging out her washing,' he said. 'A taxi just drove by.' A few moments passed. 'Andrew's riding his new bike and the Coopers are having sex.' Thomas and Melanie shot up in bed. 'How do you know that?' demanded Thomas. 'Their kid is standing out on the balcony too,' his son replied.

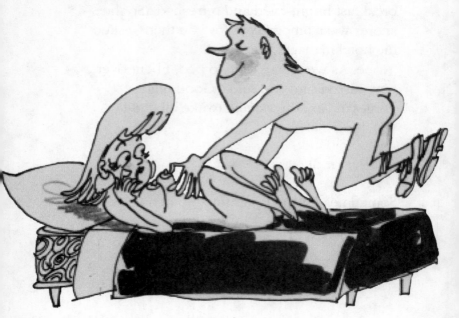

★

Adam came first. But then, men always do.

Cheng Fut ran a takeaway Chinese store in the red light district. Girls were always coming into the store in their skimpy clothes, telling each other about their last customer and swapping penis size stories. Cheng Fut became so horny one evening he bolted home as soon as he had served his last meal of the day.
'How about a 69?' he asked his wife.
'Are you joking?' she said grumpily. 'Why in hell would I want braised beef in black bean sauce at this time of night?'

An old man with chest pains visits his doctor.
'You are very ill,' says the doctor. 'There must be no smoking, no drinking, and no sex.'
'I can't live like that!' protests the old man.
'Okay,' says the doctor, 'have one cigarette a day, and one glass of wine.'
'What about sex?' asks the old man.
'Only with your wife,' replies the doctor. 'You need to avoid all excitement.'

10 REASONS WHY CHOCOLATE IS BETTER THAN SEX

1. You can *get* chocolate.

2. You can share chocolate with a group of friends without being considered obscene.

3. Chocolate satisfies even when it has gone soft.

4. You can have chocolate in front of your parents.

5. If you bite the nuts too hard the chocolate won't mind.

6. Two people of the same sex can have chocolate without being called nasty names.

7. The word 'commitment' doesn't scare off chocolate.

8. You can have chocolate in your office without upsetting your colleagues.

9. Chocolate isn't ugly, hairy or smelly.

10. A big piece of chocolate is of course better, but even a small piece satisfies.

★

PLAYING THE SAX

Do I have to be married to play sax safely?
*No, although married people play the sax,
many single people play the sax with complete
strangers every day.*

My parents say they didn't play the sax until
they were 18. How old do you think someone
should be, before they can play sax?
*Sax playing is better left until adulthood –
the necessary organs are at that stage better
developed.*

There is an area in the neighbourhood where
you can go and pay for sax lessons. Is this
legal?
*Yes. Many people have no other way of
learning to play sax and must pay a
professional to teach them.*

Should a cover always be used for the sax?
*Unless you are really sure of the person who
last used your sax, a cover should always be
used to ensure safe sax.*

What happens if I get nervous and play sax
prematurely?
*DON'T PANIC! Many people prematurely play
sax when they are young. Just wait until
you're older before you try again.*

★

A well-to-do Englishman found himself walking in a neighbourhood a class or two below his own. It happened to be a windy day and as he passed a young woman the wind caught her skirt and lifted it above her head. 'Oh, it's airy, isn't it?' said the man. The young woman replied, 'Yeah, what did you expect? Feathers?'

★

Two old ladies are sitting in a park, when a flasher walks up, yanks open his raincoat and exposes himself totally to them. His penis is just hanging right out there, all big, ugly and hairy. This is an enormous shock to the ladies and one of them has a stroke right away! But the other one can't quite reach.

★

As the old farmer lay dying his wife held his hand and murmured sweet things in his ear. The farmer, using the last ounce of energy he had, said, 'Mary, you've been with me through all my bad times. When all my cows died, you were there. When Oakey, the best dog ever to have chased sheep, was run over by a tractor and killed, you were there. And when I fell into the water drum and almost drowned, you were there too. And now that I am about to leave this earth, you are still here. You know what Mary? I'm beginning to think you're bad luck!'

A little old woman walks into a sex shop. She goes up to the counter and says, 'Ex-ex-ex-excuse m-me, y-y-young m-man, b-b-b-but d-d-d-do y-you s-sell v-v-v-vibrators?'
'Why yes we do.'
She holds her hands about 18 inches apart and says, 'D-d-d-d-do y-y-you h-h-h-have a-a-any o-o-ones ab-b-bout th-th-this l-l-long?'
'Why yes we do.'
'W-w-w-well t-t-ell m-m-m-me, h-h-h-how d-d-do y-y-y-ou t-t-t-turn it-t-t o-o-o-off?'

Johnno is a handsome guy, and recently he
started going out with the most attractive girl in
the neighbourhood. The only problem he has
is his lips – they seemed to always be chapped
and dry, and now that he was going out with
such a stunner, he made sure he carried a jar
of vaseline with him so he could keep his lips
moistened. Anyway, one day his girlfriend
suggests he meet her parents over dinner, so he
goes over to her place in his best clothes.
When he gets there, he finds her waiting for
him in the front yard.

'No matter what happens tonight, don't say a
word,' she warns. 'Our family hates cleaning
up. Whoever speaks first at dinner tonight will
have to clean the house, and that would not
be fun!' She then leads him into the house,
where he is hit by the most incredible smell.
Piles upon piles of rubbish lie on the floor.
Empty milk cartons, chip packets, broken
eggshells, banana skins...the place looks like a
rubbish truck has dropped its entire load in the
middle of the loungeroom. His girlfriend takes
him into the dining room, where he nods at
the parents, who nod back. They start the
meal, and nobody says anything at all. So
Johnno decides to have a little fun. He grabs
his girlfriend, throws her down on the table
and has wild sex with her in front of her
parents. His girlfriend is embarrassed, her dad

wildly angry, and her mum horrified when they sit back down, but no one says a word. A few minutes later he grabs her mum, throws her on the table and does a repeat performance. Now his girlfriend is furious, her dad is boiling, and the mother incredibly shocked. But still there is complete silence at the table. All of a sudden Johnno starts feeling a little nervous about what he has done, and his mouth becomes dry. He takes the vaseline out of his pocket, smears it on his fingers and is just about to apply it to his lips when the girlfriend's father frantically jumps up and screams, 'OKAY, OKAY, I'LL DO THE F***ING DISHES!'

DICTIONARY ENTRIES

Bitch   (bich) n.
female: The woman who stole your boyfriend.
male: The hot, sexy chick at reception.

Butt (but) n.
female: The body part that every item of clothing makes 'look bigger.'
male: The organ of mooning, farting, and number two-ing.

Commitment (ko-mit-ment) n.
female: The desire to marry and raise a family.
male: A female-specific term; not relevant to the male species.

Communication (ko-myoo-ni-kay-shun) n.
female: The open sharing of thoughts and feelings with one's partner.
male: The sharing of dirty jokes with one's mates.

Entertainment
(en-ter-tayn-ment) n.
female: A good movie, concert, play or book.
male: Anything involving alcohol, table tops, and women dressed in material only half an inch in width.

Flatulence
(flach-u-lents) n.
female:
A by-product
of digestion.
male: An endless
source of entertainment,
self-expression and
male bonding.

Making love (may-king luv) n.
female: The greatest expression of intimacy a couple can achieve.
male: What men have to call 'boinking' to get women to boink.

Needs (need-z) n.
female: The delicate balance of emotional, physical and psychological longing one seeks to have fulfilled in a relationship.
male: Food, sex and beer.

Taste (tayst) v.
female: Something you do frequently to whatever you're cooking, to make sure it's good.
male: Something you must do to anything you think has gone bad, prior to tossing it out.

Thingy (thing-ee) n.
female: Any part under a car's hood.
male: Any part of the female anatomy.

Vulnerable (vul-ne-ra-bull) adj.
female: Fully opening up one's self emotionally to another.
male: Playing footy without a ball protector.

★

A primary school teacher thought it would be interesting for her students to learn to identify different names for the various kinds of meats. One day, she cooked up several different meats and labelled them. As each student took a bite they were asked to identify the animal. Little Rani took a bite of the meat labelled beef and correctly said that it came from a cow. Jared took a bite of pork and also correctly identified the meat as coming from a pig. The last meat was labelled venison. The children chewed and chewed and after numerous incorrect guesses the teacher attempted to give them a hint. 'What does your mummy call your daddy when he comes home from work at night?' she asked. All of a sudden little Joey jumped up from the back of the classroom and yelled, 'Jesus Christ! Spit it out! It's Arsehole!'

Familiarity breeds children.

Cinderella had been invited to a ball but her wicked stepmother was being a bitch and reminded her that she did not have the right clothes, and she sure as hell wasn't going to buy her any. Cinderella sat about looking glum, until suddenly her Fairy Godmother appeared with some good news: she would give Cinderella a beautiful dress and matching shoes as long as Cinderella met her two conditions. The first condition was that she had to wear a diaphragm. Cinderella's mouth dropped open and she said, 'You must be crazy! I'm on the Pill, I don't need to wear a diaphragm.' When the Fairy Godmother reminded Cinderella that the alternative was to sit at home watching *Neighbours*, Cinderella agreed to wear one. 'Well, what's the second condition?' Cinderella asked. The Fairy Godmother replied, 'You must be back home at midnight.' Cinderella couldn't believe this – a midnight curfew most definitely precluded getting blind drunk and raging all night. The Fairy Godmother told Cinderella that if she wasn't home by midnight, her diaphragm would turn into a pumpkin, so Cinderella again reluctantly agreed to meet this condition. At midnight though, Cinderella wasn't to be seen... at 1 a.m., no Cinderella... 3 a.m., no Cinderella... finally, at 5 a.m., Cinderella showed up at the door with a huge smirk on her face. The Fairy Godmother looked angrily at Cinderella and said, 'Where the hell have you been? Your diaphragm was supposed to turn into a pumpkin five hours ago!' Cinderella told the Fairy Godmother all about the wonderful Prince she had met and how he had taken care of it for her. The Fairy Godmother had never heard of a Prince having such powers and asked Cinderella for his name. She replied, 'I can't remember exactly, but it was Peter Peter something or other...'

★

The old man walked slowly into the clinic.
'You gotta help me, Doc,' he said. 'You've got
to help me lower my sex drive.'
'C'mon, who are you kidding?' said the doctor.
'We both know that your sex drive is all in
your head.'
'That's what I mean. You've got to do some-
thing to lower it!'

★

A city lad was tearing through the country one day in his new car when out of nowhere appeared a bull on the road. Unable to avoid it, the lad drove right into it, killing it instantly. Feeling very guilty, he walked over to the farmhouse and knocked on the door. 'I'm so sorry, madam, I've killed your bull. I'd very much like to replace him.'

'Oh, okay,' replied the farmer's wife. 'Go around to the side and you'll find the cows in the barn.'

A man from the city was driving along in the country when he came across a farmer sowing the fields without any trousers. 'How come you're not wearing any trousers?' he asked in astonishment. 'Well, mate, the other day I went out into the field and I forgot to wear my shirt. That night my neck was stiffer than a door. So this is my wife's idea.'

What do men have in common with a toilet seat, anniversaries and a clitoris? *They always miss them.*

★

It was Sam the Milkman's last day on the job after 40 years of delivering milk to the same neighbourhood. When he arrived at the first house on his route he was greeted by the whole family, who congratulated him for his many years of good work and sent him on his way with an envelope filled with money. At the second house he was presented with a box of fine cigars. The folks at the third house handed him some fine Swiss chocolates and some vintage red wine. At the fourth house he was met at the door by a strikingly beautiful woman in a revealing negligee. She took him by the hand, led him through the door and took him upstairs to the bedroom where they had the most passionate sex he had ever experienced. Afterwards they went downstairs, where she fixed him a giant breakfast: eggs, bacon, pancakes, and freshly squeezed orange juice. When he was truly full she poured him a cup of steaming coffee. As she was pouring, he noticed a dollar bill sitting on the table, with his name written on a piece of paper right next to it. 'All this is just too wonderful for words,' he said, 'but what's the dollar for?'

'Well,' she replied, 'last night, I told my husband that today would be your last day, and that we should do something special for you. I asked him what to give you. He said, "F*** him, give him a dollar." The breakfast was my idea.'

★

The census taker told the sheriff of a country town that there was something wrong with the population figures. 'For the last ten years the population had been the same: 2058.'

'Yeah, that's right,' said the sheriff. 'It's always been 2058.'

'But surely some one has a baby every so often?'

'Sure,' replied the sheriff. 'And every time it happens some bloke has to leave town.'

★

A man had decided to see a prostitute for the first time, but when he went to the address his mate had told him about, it looked like the place had shut down. 'Hey,' he yelled. 'I want to come in.'

'Okay, then put $100 through the mail slot.' He did. But nothing happened and no one came out. 'Hey, I want to be screwed!'

'What?' called out a woman's voice. 'Again?'

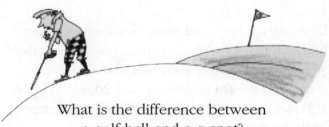

What is the difference between
a golf ball and a g-spot?
*A man will spend 20 minutes
looking for a golf ball.*

'What do you think, Roger,' began Andy.
'Is it okay to talk to your wife when you
make love?'
'Oh I guess it would be all right,' replied Roger
thoughtfully. 'If there's a phone by the bed.'

★

One night a husband came home to his wife with a black eye.

'What happened to you?' she asked.

'I got into a fight with the landlord. He said he had slept with every woman in this apartment building except for one.'

'Hmm,' his wife replied. 'I bet it's that ugly woman on the second floor.'

Frustrated by her husband's insistence that they make love in the dark, a wife switched on her bedlight one night in the middle of a romp – only to find a cucumber in his hand.

'Is THIS,' she asked, pointing to the vegetable, 'what you've been using on me for the last five years?'

'Honey, let me explain ...'

'Why, you impotent bastard!' she screamed. 'You cheating son of a –.'

'Cheating huh?!' interrupted her husband indignantly. 'Perhaps you'd care to explain our three kids?'

'How many wives have you had?' Mr Trent
asked Mr Kadie. 'Five,' replied Mr Kadie. 'But
only one of them was my own.'

★

A woman was in hospital, going through the
final stages of labor. As she was experiencing
quite a bit of pain, their doctor asked the
husband if he'd like to participate in the
birthing process and take some of the pain
away from his wife. The husband agreed, so
the doctor got out a strange machine with a red

lever. He set the lever to 10 percent, telling the husband that even 10 percent was probably more pain than he'd ever experienced. But the man didn't feel a thing. Being the egotistical guy that he was, he was sure that he could handle as much pain as his wife so he insisted that the doctor crank the lever up to 100 percent. After it was over, the man stood up, stretched a little. Both he and his wife felt great. Later, when they took the baby home, they found the milkman dead on their doorstep.

★

What are the three words you don't want to
hear while making love?
'Honey, I'm home.'

★

A man rang home in the early afternoon one
day to speak to his wife. The maid answered
the phone and told him that she was upstairs
in the bedroom with her boyfriend. After rant-
ing and raving for a minute, the man asked the
maid if she'd like to make a quick $10,000.
'Sure,' she said enthusiastically. 'What do I
have to do?'

'Take the gun from my desk and shoot both of them.' The maid went upstairs and did as she had been instructed. She came back down the stairs, picked up the phone, and said, 'Now what do I do with the bodies?' The man said, 'Take them out the back and throw them in the pool.'

'What pool?' asked the maid. After a moment of silence, the man said, 'Is this 9321 4674?'

Two business men, working away from home a lot, decided to share a mistress. They set her up in her own apartment, sharing the expenses equally between them. One day the mistress told the two men she was pregnant. Wanting to do the right thing, the men agreed to split the costs of bringing up the child.

When the mistress went into hospital, only one of the businessmen was in town to be there for the birth of the baby. When the other one returned, he went to the hospital to visit the newborn. His friend was sitting on the hospital steps looking depressed. 'What's wrong? Were there problems with the birth?'

'Oh, she's fine, but I have some bad news. She had twins, and mine died.'

A man, somewhat sceptical, went to see a gypsy fortune teller. 'I see you are the father of two children,' began the gypsy.
'Great, I knew this was all nonsense. I'm actually the father of three children.'
'That's what you think,' smiled the gypsy.

★

One evening a boy sat down to say his prayers before going to bed. His father walked past at this moment and paused to listen. 'God bless Mummy and Daddy and Grandpa. And bye bye Grandma.' The father thought this was a little strange, but thought nothing more of it until the next day when Grandma had a heart attack and died. A week later, he happened to overhear his son again saying his prayers, and listened more intently this time. 'God bless Mummy and Daddy. Goodbye Grandpa.' Sure enough, the next day Grandpa suffered a stroke and died instantly. A month later, once again the father heard his son praying. 'God bless Mummy. Bye bye Daddy.' The father was mortified. He went to work, but was too scared to do anything in case he had an accident. When he got home from work, he told his wife what an awfully worrying day he'd had. His wife simply scoffed. 'You think you've had it bad? I've had a terrible day. I got up this morning and opened the front door to discover the postie lying dead in the front yard.'

★

One day this guy called Ari died. When he arrived to be judged, he was told that he had cheated on his income taxes, and therefore would not be allowed to go to Heaven unless he spent the next five years with a 200 kilogram, stupid, ugly woman. Ari decided that this was a small price to pay for an eternity in Heaven. So off he went with this enormous, vile woman. As they were walking along, he saw his friend Matty ahead. Matty was with a big, incredibly ugly woman too. When he approached Matty he asked him what was going on, and Matty replied, 'I cheated on my income taxes.' They both shook their heads in understanding and figured that as long as they have to be with these women, they might as well hang out together to make it easier to bear. So the four of them were walking along, minding their own business when Ari and Matty could have sworn that they saw their friend Nick up ahead, only this man was with an absolutely gorgeous centrefold. Stunned, Ari and Matty approached the man and in fact it was their friend Nick. They asked him how he had managed to land this unbelievable goddess, while they were stuck with these god-awful women. Nick replied, 'I have no idea, and I'm definitely not complaining. This has been absolutely the best time of my life, and I have had five years of the best sex any man could hope to look forward to. There is only one thing that I can't seem to understand. After every time we have sex, she rolls over and murmurs to herself, "Damn income taxes!!"'

★

If a man is alone in the woods talking to himself, with no women around for miles, is he STILL wrong?

★

Adam had been going out with Sally for several months, but still had not managed to sleep with her. One night he tried to cajole her into it. 'But I'm afraid to,' she said. 'Won't you lose respect for me in the morning?'
'Of course not,' he reassured her. 'Provided you're good at it.'

★

What's the difference between a woman and a battery?
A battery has a positive side.

One day upon arriving home from work, Anton's wife informed him she was interested in having breast enlargement surgery. When he asked why, she said, 'Because it will make me more attractive to you.'
He asked her how much the operation was, and she replied, '$4,000 per breast.' He exclaimed, '$4,000 per breast?! That's ridiculous. We can't afford that! Have you tried the toilet paper method?' She looked puzzled. 'Sure — each night before you go to bed, rub toilet paper between your breasts, and over a period of time, they should grow.' She said, 'That won't work!'
Anton replied, 'It worked on your arse!'

CLASSES FOR MEN

1. How to Find the Vacuum

2. Yes, We Call that an Iron

3. If You Want Her to Wear Sexy Underwear, You've Got To Pay For It

4. Understanding the Female Response to Your Coming Home Late

5. You – The Weaker Sex

6. Drooling at Other Women – Yes There is a Cure

7. PMT – Feel It, Cry About It, Offer Sympathy

8. How to Stay Awake After Sex

9. The Rubbish Bin – Taking it Out

10. How to Wrap Your Own Sandwiches

11. Watching the Footy All Weekend is Not Fun

12. Bragging About No. Twos – How Not To

13. Remote Control 101 – Overcoming Your Dependency

14. Remote Control 102 – It Lives Not on the TV

15. Romanticism – Ideas other Than Sex

16. She Does Not Want to Hear Your Farts

17. Mother-in-Laws – They are People Too

18. The Art of Nappy Changing

19. Separation Anxiety – You Don't Need that Beer

20. You Too Can Host a Dinner Party

21. How to Lose that Beer Gut

22. Techniques for Calling Home

★

CLASSES FOR WOMEN

1. Are You Ready – Definition of the Word 'Yes'

2. Elementary Map Reading

3. Basic Car Mechanics

4. Shopping 101 – Going Without Your Man

5. Shopping 102 – Using Your Own Credit Card

6. Gaining Three Kilos vs the End of the World: A Study in Contrast

7. Gift-giving Fundamentals (was: Ties Bad – Pin-up Girl Calendar Good)

8. Driving 101: Introducing the Manual Transmission

9. Driving 102: Checking the Oil

10. Jealousy – Doing Without

11. How to Earn Your Own Money

12. How To Leave The Toilet Seat Up

13. Why It's Unacceptable To Talk About the Menstrual Cycle During Lunch

14. Nagging – An Evil Word

15. Sex is Not a Forum for Playing Dead

16. Silence: Where No Woman Has Gone Before

17. The Undiscovered Side of Banking – Deposits

18. Gossip Sessions – Stop Being a Bitch

19. Telephone Skills – How to Hang Up

20. Water Retention – Fact or Fat

21. Sex – It's For Married Couples Too

Two deaf men were discussing their night out the previous evening. The first man said, 'My wife was asleep when I got home, so I was able to sneak into bed, and not get into trouble.'
The second deaf man said, 'Boy you're lucky. My wife was wide awake, waiting for me in bed, and she started swearing at me and giving me hell for being out so late.'
The first deaf man asked, 'So what did you do?'
'I turned out the light,' the second man replied.

Seems God was ahead of schedule in creating the universe and had a bit of spare time and a few leftover things to play with, so he dropped in to visit Adam and Eve. He told the couple that one of the things he had to give away was the ability to stand up and pee. 'It's a very handy thing,' God told the couple.

Adam popped a cork. Jumped up and begged, 'Oh, give that to me! I'd love to be able to do that! Oh please, oh please, oh please, let me have that ability. It'd be great! I'm working in the garden, and instead of running to the loo, I could just pull it out, it'd be so cool. Oh please, God, let it be me who you give that gift to, let me stand and pee, oh please...' On and on he went like an excited little boy (who had to pee). Eve just smiled and shook her head at the display. She told God that if Adam really wanted it so badly, and it sure seemed to be the sort of thing that would make him happy, she really wouldn't mind if God gave it to him. 'Fine,' God said, and the deed was done. He looked again into his bag of leftover gifts. 'Now, what else is here? Oh yes, multiple orgasms...'

★

AAH!

DOING IT

Help desk people tell you how to do it, hang up the phone, and laugh at you with their co-workers.

Firemen do it with a big hose.

Crooks do it with a gun in their pocket.

Telemarketers do it with their mouths.

Physicists do it with a big bang.

Pet shop owners do it with hamsters.

Consultants tell you how to do it, charge you a fortune, but never actually do it themselves.

Spies do it under cover.

Statisticians are 95% confident that they do it.

Hackers do it with bugs.

Mortgage bankers do it with interest.

Radio operators do it with frequency.

Blondes do it with anyone.

Landlords do it every 1st of the month.

Golfers do it in 18 holes.

Deepsea divers do it under extreme pressure.

Radio DJs do it on request.

★

DISADVANTAGES OF BOY SUPERHEROES

They'd much rather stay in and play Doom than go out on patrol.

They blush and stutter when confronted by a female supervillain.

They pick their noses when you're with the FBI.

They go into a sulk if you won't play Dungeons and Dragons with them.

When they've caught a villain, they sound silly when they say, 'Stick them up, dude!'

When they pull out their gun, it sometimes has old bubble gum stuck to it.

They think it's funny to suddenly fart in public.

They can easily be taunted by supervillains.

They get carsick in the Crimemobile.

It doesn't sound too convincing yelling, 'Stop or die!' when their voice breaks mid-sentence.

DISADVANTAGES OF GIRL SUPERHEROES

They're always holding slumber parties in the Crimecave.

One tiny zit and they won't leave the house.

They insist on criminals not seeing them in the same clothes twice.

They won't fight crime if X-Files is on.

They won't fight crime if they're waiting for a phone call from that cute guy they met a few days ago.

Batman or Spiderman may try to steal her away from you.

They kill people when they're premenstrual.

They won't use their fists to fight supervillains in case they break a nail.

They get crushes on villians because 'He's like so totally dark an' mysterious an' moody.'

If they're having a bad hair day, forget it.

Corey and Ben were sharing a few beers at the pub. 'So how come you and your girl broke up?' asked Ben. Corey was rather quiet. 'Sickness,' was all he said. 'I don't remember either of you being sick.' Corey shrugged. 'It was sickness. I just got sick of her, that's all.'

Two blokes were talking about Freudian slips. 'I made the worst Freudian slip last night,' said the first bloke. 'What was it?' asked the other. 'Well, the wife and I were having dinner and I meant to say, "Please pass the salt," but instead, by mistake...it just slipped out of my mouth: "YOU'RE RUINING MY LIFE YOU F***ING BITCH!"'

James told his girlfriend, 'There's one word you could say that would make me the happiest bloke around when I ask you the question, will you marry me?'
'No,' said the girl.
'Thanks,' said James. 'That was the word.'

How many men does it take to change a roll of toilet paper?
I don't know. It's never happened.

★

A couple go to a bull auction in the country one weekend. The auctioneer begins his spiel for the first bull. He says, 'A fine specimen, this bull reproduced 60 times last year.'

The wife nudges her husband and says, 'Wow — more than five times a month!'

The auctioneer then calls out, 'Another fine specimen, this bull reproduced 120 times last year.'

Again the wife nudges her husband. 'Hey, that's some 10 times a month. What do you say about that?!'

Her husband is getting really annoyed with this comparison. The third bull is up for sale: 'And this extraordinary specimen reproduced 365 times last year!'

The wife slaps her husband on the arm and yells, 'That's once a day! How about YOU?!'

The husband was pretty irritated by now, and yells back, 'Big deal, once a day! I bet he didn't have to do it with the same cow!'

★

10 REJECTION LINES GIVEN BY WOMEN (AND WHAT THEY ACTUALLY MEAN)

1. I think of you as a brother. (And Mum says I shouldn't do that with him anymore.)

2. I prefer older men. (Or at least, ones that don't still live with their parents.)

3. I need some time to sort my feelings out. (I want to see if there is anyone better out there.)

4. I'm not attracted to you in 'that' way. (You ugly bastard.)

5. My life is too complicated right now. (I don't want you spending the whole night because my boyfriend will be back home soon.)

6. I need time to myself. (How else am I going to find a hunky guy?)

7. I'm married. (Also separated, but you don't need to know that.)

8. It's not you, it's me. (It's not me, it's you.)

9. I'm celibate. (At least, I am when you're around.)

10. Let's be friends. (I know you're good with cars.)

★

10 REJECTION LINES GIVEN BY MEN (AND WHAT THEY ACTUALLY MEAN)

1. I think of you as a sister. (You're ugly.)

2. I prefer older women. (You're ugly.)

3. I need some time to sort my feelings out. (You're ugly.)

4. I'm not attracted to you in 'that' way. (You're ugly.)

5. My life is too complicated right now. (You're ugly.)

6. I need time to myself. (You're ugly.)

7. I'm married. (You're ugly.)

8. It's not you, it's me. (You're ugly.)

9. I'm celibate. (You're ugly.)

10. Let's be friends. (You're ugly.)

TOP 10 DATING TIPS FOR WOMEN

1. Enjoy talking about football. It's a very intellectual game.

2. Learn the precise art of pouring a beer. And then pour many.

3. Bring your own jacket.

4. Don't make him hold your purse.

5. Shopping is not fascinating.

6. Men don't want to talk about marriage on the first date. Or after the first year. Or at all.

7. Don't act clucky when you see little kids.

8. When he asks for a threesome with you and your best friend, he is only joking.

9. Unless the answer is yes. In which case, can he videotape it?

10. And show his mates the next day?

★

DATING DEFINITIONS

Dating: The process of spending lots of money and time in order to sleep with someone.

Easy: A term used to describe a woman who behaves like a man.

Eye contact: Used to signal interest. Many women have difficulty looking a man directly in the eyes, not due to shyness, but because a woman's eyes are not located in her chest.

A friend: A person who is flawed in such a way as to rule them out for dating purposes.

Indifference: A woman's feeling towards a man, which is interpreted by the man as 'playing hard to get.'

One night stand: What you call a date where you really like somebody and want to start a relationship, but they don't like you enough to bother ringing again.

Nymphomaniac: A man's term for a woman who wants to do it more often than he does.

Love at first sight: What you experience on the basis of looks alone before you actually realise what a loser the other person is.

Law of relativity: How attractive a given person appears to be is directly proportionate to how drunk you are.

15 REASONS WHY IT IS BETTER BEING A WOMAN

1. Free drinks.

2. Free dinners.

3. You can hug your friend without wondering if she thinks you're gay.

4. You know The Truth about whether size matters.

5. Speeding ticket? Why officer, what's that?

6. You've never experienced walking around school with a jumper strategically placed in front of your crotch.

7. Condoms do not affect your enjoyment of sex.

8. You can sleep your way to the top.

9. Nothing crucial can be cut off with one clean sweep.

10. It's possible to live your whole life without taking a group shower.

11. If you cheat on your boyfriend, people assume it's because you've been emotionally neglected.

12. You'll never have to punch a hole through anything with your fist.

13. You can quickly end any fight by crying.

14. You're allowed to be afraid of spiders and other creepy crawlies.

15. You can talk to people of the opposite sex without picturing them naked.

One day Gerry asks Fiona out to a movie. She accepts and they have a pretty good time. A few nights later he asks her out to dinner and again they enjoy themselves. They continue to see each other regularly and after a while neither of them is seeing anyone else.
And then one evening when they're driving home, a thought occurs to Fiona and without really thinking she says it out aloud: 'Do you realise that as of tonight, we've been seeing each other for exactly six months?'

And then there is silence in the car.
To Fiona it seems like a very loud silence.

She thinks to herself:

Geez, I wonder if it bothers him that I said that. Maybe he's been feeling confined by our relationship; maybe he thinks I'm trying to push him into some kind of obligation that he doesn't want, or isn't sure of.

And Gerry is thinking:

Gosh. Six months.

And Fiona is thinking:

But hey, I'm not sure I want this kind of relationship either. Sometimes I wish I had a little more space, so I'd have time to think about whether I really want us to keep going the way we are, moving steadily toward... I mean, where are we going? Are we just going to keep seeing each other at this level of intimacy? Are we heading toward marriage? Toward children? Toward a lifetime together? Am I ready for that level of commitment? Do I really even know this person?

And Gerry is thinking:

So...that means it was...let's see...it was February when we started going out, which was right after I had the car at the dealer's

which means...let me check the odometer...
Whoa! I am way overdue for an oil
change here.

And Fiona is thinking:

He's upset. I can see it on his face. Maybe I'm
reading this completely wrong. Maybe he
wants more from our relationship, more
intimacy, more commitment. Maybe he has
sensed – even before I sensed it – that I was
feeling some reservations. Yes, I bet that's it.
That's why he's so reluctant to say anything
about his own feelings. He's afraid of being
rejected.

And Gerry is thinking:

...And I'm gonna have them take a look at the
transmission again. I don't care what those
morons say, it's still not working right. And
they better not try to blame it on the cold
weather this time. What cold weather? It's 30
degrees out and this thing is shifting like a
damn garbage truck – and I paid those
incompetent thieves $800.

And Fiona is thinking:

He's angry. And I don't blame him – I'd be
angry too. I feel so guilty putting him through
this, but I can't help the way I feel. I'm just
not sure.

And Gerry is thinking:

They'll probably say it's only a 90-day warranty. That's exactly what they're gonna say, the scumbags.

And Fiona is thinking:

Maybe I'm just too idealistic, waiting for a knight to come riding up on his white horse, when I'm sitting next to a perfectly good person. A person I enjoy being with, a person I truly do care about, a person who seems to truly care about me. A person who is in pain because of my romantic fantasy.

And Gerry is thinking:

Warranty? I'll give them a damn warranty. I'll take their warranty and stick it up their ...

'Gerry?' Fiona says.
'What?' says Gerry, startled.
'Please don't torture yourself like this,' says Fiona, her eyes beginning to brim with tears.
'Maybe I should never have... I feel so...' She breaks down sobbing.
'What?' says Gerry.
'I'm such a fool,' Fiona sobs. 'I mean, I know there's no knight. I really know that. There's no knight, and there's no horse.'
'There's no knight? No horse?' says Gerry, baffled.

'You think I'm a fool, don't you?' Fiona says.

'No!' says Gerry, playing it safe.

'It's just that...it's just that I... I need more time,' says Fiona. There is a fifteen second pause while Gerry, thinking as fast as he can, tries to think of a safe response. Finally he comes with one that he thinks might work.

'Yes,' he says.

Fiona, deeply moved, touches his hand. 'Oh Gerry, do you really feel that way?' she says.

'What way?' says Gerry.

'That way about time,' says Fiona.

'Oh,' says Gerry, glancing at his watch. 'No. I mean, yes.'

Fiona turns to face him and gazes deeply into his eyes, causing him to become very nervous about what she might say next, especially if it involves a horse. At last she speaks. 'Thank you, Gerry,' she says.

'Er, yeah,' says Gerry uncertainly.

Then he takes her home and she lies on her bed, a conflicted, tortured soul, and weeps until dawn. Whereas when Gerry gets back to his place, he opens a bag of potato chips, turns on the TV and immediately becomes deeply involved in a re-run of a tennis match between two Czechoslovakians he has never heard of. A tiny voice in the far recesses of his mind tells him that something major was going on back there in the car, but he is pretty sure there is no way he would ever understand what, and so he figures it's better if he doesn't think about it. This is also Gerry's policy regarding world hunger.

The next day Fiona will call her closest friend, or perhaps two of them and they will talk about this situation for six straight hours. In painstaking detail, they will analyse everything she said and everything he said, going over it time and time again, exploring every word, expression and gesture for nuances of meaning, considering every possible ramification. They will continue to discuss this subject on and off, for weeks, maybe months, never reaching any definite conclusions, but never getting bored with it either.

Meanwhile, Gerry, while playing tennis one day with a mutual friend of his and Fiona's, will pause just before serving, frown and say, 'Scott? Did Fiona ever ride a horse at night?'

★

25 THINGS NOT TO SAY DURING SEX

1. But everybody looks funny naked!

2. You woke me up for that?

3. Try breathing through your nose.

4. Is that a Medic-Alert Pendant?

5. But whipped cream makes me break out.

6. On second thought, let's turn off the lights.

7. I thought you had the keys to the handcuffs!

8. I want a baby!

9. What is *that?*

10. Maybe we should call Dr. Ruth...

11. Did you know the ceiling needs painting?

12. I think you have it on backwards.

13. Did I remember to take my pill?

14. I told you it wouldn't work without batteries!

15. Did I tell you my Aunt Martha died in this bed?

16. No, really... I do this part better myself!

17. Perhaps you're just out of practice.

18. What tampon?

19. I have a confession...

20. I really hate people who actually think sex means something!

21. Did you come yet, dear?

22. I'll tell you who I'm fantasising about if you tell me who you're fantasising about...

23. When would you like to meet my parents?

24. Long kisses clog my sinuses...

25. Was *what* good for me?

15 RULES THAT GUYS WISH GIRLS KNEW

1. If you think you're fat, you probably are. Don't ask us.

2. Learn to work the toilet seat: if it's up put it down.

3. Sometimes, he's not thinking about you. Live with it.

4. Don't ask him what he's thinking about unless you are prepared to discuss such topics as navel lint, his latest software purchase and four wheel drives.

5. Get rid of your cat. And no, it's not different; it's just like every other cat.

6. Anything you wear is fine. Really.

7. No, he doesn't know when your anniversary is. Males don't have that innate ability for marking dates on calendars.

8. Your mother doesn't have to be our best friend.

9. Foreign films are best left to foreigners.

10. It is neither in your best interest nor ours to take the quiz together.

11. If something we said could be interpreted two ways, and one of the ways makes you sad and angry, we meant the other one.

12. Whenever possible, please say whatever you have to say during commercials.

13. Women wearing Wonderbras and low-cut blouses lose their right to complain about having their boobs stared at.

14. The relationship is never going to be like it was the first two months we were going out.

15. Don't ask if we're attracted to your friends. Of course we are.

An old man of 90 years marries a lovely woman three times younger, and they are on their honeymoon. Because the woman is worried about her new husband exerting himself she tells him they should have separate suites. That night a knock comes on her door and her groom is ready for action. They unite in conjugal union and all goes well whereupon he takes his leave of her and she prepares to go to sleep for the night.

After a few minutes there's a knock on the door and there the old guy is again, ready for more action. Somewhat surprised she consents to further coupling which is again successful after which he bids her a fond good night and leaves.

She is certainly ready for slumber at this point and is close to sleep for the second time when there is another knock at the door and there he is again, as fresh as someone her own age and ready for more. Once again they do the horizontal tango. As they're lying in afterglow the young bride says to him, 'I am really impressed that a guy your age has enough juice to go for it three times. I've been with guys half your age who could only manage to do it once.'

The old guy looks puzzled and turns to her and says, 'Was I already here?'

★

Dumb, Blonde and Stupid

Laugh alone and the world thinks you're an idiot.

★

What do you call someone who hangs out with musicians?
A drummer.

★

What does it mean when a drummer is drooling out of both sides of his mouth?
The stage is level.

The light at the end of the tunnel is an oncoming freight train.

What's long and hard on a drummer?
The third grade.

Judge:	Do you know how many months pregnant you are right now?
Woman:	I will be three months on the first of December.
Judge:	So the date of conception was the first of September?
Woman:	Yes.
Judge:	What were you and your husband doing at that time?

A popular rock band began a tour of the world, hoping to gain some new fans and sell a lot of records. The band's first destination was Scotland. As they had some time to kill before their first gig, the two drummers of the band went on a day trip to Edinburgh. They soon began arguing about how to pronounce it. 'It's "Ed-in-burra",' said the first one. 'No way, you pronounce it "Ed-in-berg",' said the second. To settle it once and for all they decided to ask a local. Stopping at a hamburger joint, they asked the girl behind the counter, 'How do you pronounce the name of this place?' She looked at them strangely for a minute, then said slowly and carefully, 'Mac-don-alds.'

A blonde needed to send a message to her mother who was overseas. She went into the communications centre, but was told it would cost $50. She said, 'I'm desperate to talk to Mum, but I don't have any money. Please, I'll do anything for you if you would help me!' The man arched an eyebrow. 'Anything?' 'Yes, anything,' promised the blonde. So the man took her into a room down the hall and shut the door. Then he said, 'Get down on your knees.' She did. Then he said, 'Undo my zipper.' She did. Then he said, 'Now take out my willy.' She took it out and grabbed hold of it with both hands. The man closed his eyes, and whispered, 'Okay, go for it!'

The blonde slowly brought her mouth closer to his willy, and while holding it close to her lips, she said... 'Hello, mum?'

Why do blondes take the pill?
So they know which day of the week it is.

Why are blondes so attractive to men?
God had to give them something good to compensate for their lack of intelligence.

How does a blonde turn on the light after sex?
She opens the car door.

Why did the blonde stare at the orange juice bottle for two hours?
Because it said 'Concentrate'.

★

After several hours of exhausting acrobatic sex with an amorous blonde he had met at a bar, a man goes to the fridge to get something to drink. He pours himself a glass of milk and just before drinking it, he realises his manhood is still red-hot, so he dunks it in the glass to cool it down. Just then the blonde walks in and says, 'Oh, I always wondered how you refilled those.'

★

What's the first thing a blonde does when she wakes up?
She goes home.

What happened to the blonde who took an IQ test?
The results were negative.

A blonde started her first day at her new school with a pair of headphones on. Her teacher, realising how difficult it was starting a new school, did not want to embarrass the girl so said nothing. The next day, and the next day though, the blonde continued to wear the headphones. Finally the teacher asked her to take the headphones off. She refused. He let the issue rest for a while but as another week went on and she still wore them he called her aside after class and demanded that she remove them. She looked at him sullenly and said nothing. Exasperated, he ripped them off, whereupon she immediately fell to the floor, dead. After the ambulance had taken her body away, he picked up the headphones to see what she had been listening to. He put them on and heard, 'Breathe in ... breathe out ... breathe in .... breathe out.'

Driving down a road, a guy flashes his lights at a cute blonde he sees in the next lane and signals for her to pull over. He gets out of the car, goes over to her window and unzips his trousers. The blonde rolls her eyes and says, 'Wow, this is my fourth breathalyser test in a week!'

★

Two blondes are walking through the country.
One looks down and says, 'Hey, look at the
deer tracks.' The other blonde takes a closer
look and says, 'Those aren't deer tracks,
they're bear tracks.' The two argue back and
forth about which animal's tracks they
are, until ten minutes later when they are
hit by a train.

A blonde bought a book at the local bookstore
called *Flight to France*. She got back home
and was told it was volume four of the
encyclopaedia.

Why does a blonde keep a coathanger in the back seat of her car?
In case she locks her keys in the car.

★

Why do blondes like lightning?
They think someone is taking their picture.

★

Why do blondes hate M&Ms?
They take too long to peel.

A scantily-clad woman is sitting in a bar.
Having never shaved in her life, she has a
thick black bush of hair in each armpit. She
chugs down drinks like a man; every 10
minutes she raises her arm and flags the
bartender for another scotch. Each time she
does the other drinkers at the bar are given an
eyeful of her hairy pits. After a few hours, a
drunk at the other end of the bar says to the
bartender, 'Hey, I'd like to buy Miss Ballerina
here a drink.' The bartender replies, 'She's not
a ballerina. What makes you think she's a
ballerina?' The drunk says, 'Any girl that can lift
her leg that high *has* to be a ballerina!'

Papa Bear and Baby Bear went into the kitchen for breakfast one morning. 'Someone's eaten my porridge!' exclaimed Baby Bear. 'And someone has eaten my porridge,' grumbled Papa Bear. 'You bloody idiots!' yelled Mama Bear. 'I haven't even made the damn stuff yet.'

Why do blondes wear underwear?
So their ankles don't get cold.

What do blondes put behind their ears to attract men?
Their knees.

★

Did you hear the one about the blonde who was trapped in a shopping centre during a blackout?
She was trapped on the escalator for four hours!

★

What's the definition of mass confusion?
A room full of blondes.

★

Why do blonde girls have bruises around their belly buttons?
Because blonde guys are stupid too.

★

A pretty blonde goes out on a date to a carnival. After walking around for an hour the boy asks, 'What do you want to do now?'
'I want a weigh,' she says. So they go over to the fortune scales and weigh her. They walk around a little more and the boy asks again, 'So what do you want to do now?'
'I want a weigh,' she says. *Again?* The boy is puzzled, but takes her over to the fortune scales again. They both weigh themselves then go and grab some food.
'Now what?' asks the boy.
'I want a weigh,' says the girl.
What a weirdo, thinks the boy. *Definitely too loony for me.* He takes her over to the fortune scales again and she weighs herself for the third time, before he drives her home. As she walks into her house her sister asks, 'How was your date?'
'Wousy.'

★

What's the difference between a blonde and a trampoline?
You take your shoes off to jump on a trampoline.

★

Why does it take one million sperm to fertilise one egg?
They won't stop to ask for directions.

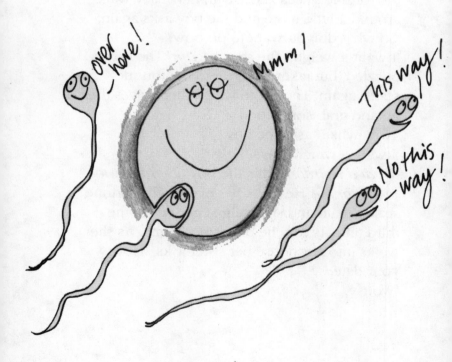

★

Two vampire bats are hanging in a tree, just before dawn, when one says to the other, 'Cor, did you hear that? My belly just rumbled. I've gotta get some more food.' His mate tells him that is far too dangerous as the sun will be up soon, but he promises to be quick, and takes off. Within a minute, he's back on the branch, blood dripping from his mouth.

'That was quick, where did you go?' asks his mate in astonishment.

'Well see that tree over there?'

'Yeah.'

'Well I didn't.'

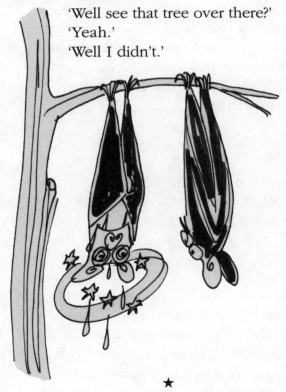

★

A blonde was suffering from constipation, so her doctor prescribed suppositories. A week later she went back to the doctor, still suffering the same problem. 'Have you been taking them regularly?' asked the doctor.
'What do you think I've been doing,' replied the blonde. 'Shoving them up my arse?'

Two blondes were walking along the train tracks one morning after spending all night at the pub. 'Wow, these stairs are killing me,' said the first blonde. The second blonde groaned back. 'The stairs don't bother me as much as the low handrail.'

Diamonds are a girl's best friend.
Dogs are a man's best friend.
So which is the dumber sex?

Three unemployed blondes were out shopping one day when they found an oil lamp in an antique store. Together they began rubbing it and miraculously, a genie appeared. 'I will grant you all as much intelligence as you desire,' said the genie. 'Wow,' said the first

blonde. 'I'd like to be ten times smarter than I am now,' and in a flash the genie granted her the wish. The next day the blonde got a job as a teacher. 'Hmmm,' said the second blonde. 'I'd like to be twenty times smarter.'
'Your wish is my command,' said the genie, as he blinked his eyes and granted her the wish. The next day she found a job as a nuclear physicist. 'Well,' said the third blonde. 'I like things the way they are. I don't have to go to a job and think all the time...if anything I'd rather be ten times dumber!'
'Righto,' said the genie, and granted her the wish. The next day she woke up and found she was a man.

DOH!

What's the definition of a blonde German?
Someone who thinks Einstein is a glass of beer.

Mein Got – it 'as a goot 'ead
on et
Ya-Vol!!

Ein Stein   Der Stein

★

How do blondes get pregnant?
And I thought blondes were dumb.

★

The blonde's husband said his wife was
obsessed with shopping. 'She's mad, she'll buy
anything that's marked down. Yesterday she
came home with an escalator.'

★

— DUMB, BLONDE AND STUPID —

What's the difference between a blonde and
a brick?
*When you lay a brick it doesn't follow you
around for three weeks whining.*

Why did the blonde stay up all night studying?
She had a urine test in the morning.

Have you heard about the blonde who had an
average IQ?
Neither has anyone else.

★

Sick and tired of being called dumb, a blonde
spent weeks and weeks learning all the capitals
for every state of Australia. The next time
someone started telling a blonde joke she said
indignantly, 'Hey, not all blondes are stupid
you know. Let me prove it. Tell me the name
of any state in Australia and I'll tell you its
capital.'
'Victoria,' someone suggested.
'V,' was her triumphant response.

One day Carl went out scuba diving. He was
15 feet below sea level when he noticed a guy
at the same depth he was, but without any
scuba gear. Carl went another further 15 feet
down, and what do you know, the guy joined
him a few minutes later. Carl was really
puzzled by this, but continued further down
yet another 15 feet. The guy caught up with
him once again. By this stage Carl couldn't
believe his eyes. He took out his waterproof
blackboard and chalked on it, 'How on earth
are you able to stay under this deep without
any scuba equipment?' The guy took the
board and chalk, scribbled over what Carl had
written, and wrote, 'I'M DROWNING, YOU
IDIOT!'

★

A nuclear scientist and a blonde are sitting on a bus together. The scientist leans over and asks if she would like to play a game. He says, 'I'll ask you a question, and if you don't know the answer, you pay me $10 and vice versa.' She's tired, so says no, but he keeps persisting. 'Look, then, you pay me $10 if you don't know the answer, and I'll pay you $100 if I don't know the answer.' He thinks that since she's a blonde he's sure to win the game. So she agrees. The scientist asks, 'How big is the Great Wall of China?' The blonde says nothing, but simply reaches into her purse and hands over $10. 'My turn now,' she says. 'What flies to the moon on Monday and returns on Thursday?' The scientist looks puzzled, and whips out his laptop computer and searches his CD encyclopaedias. He rings up all his scientific buddies and puts the word out to find an answer. Meanwhile, the blonde has fallen asleep. Some time later, when he has exhausted all his contacts and can not find the answer he nudges her awake and hands her $100. 'Well, what is the answer?' he asks her in frustration. In silence, she reaches into her bag and hands him $10.

★

A psychologist, a minister, and a scientist are walking in the forest when they come upon a little hut. As it is getting late they go into the hut and ask the man there if they can spend the night. The man obliges. 'You must be hungry,' says the hospitable man, and takes them in the kitchen, where they find a dining table standing eight feet high. They all have to jump like crazy to reach the food on the table, and are very tired by the end of the meal. 'Hmm,' says the psychologist. 'This man has obviously designed this table to act as a protective mechanism against overeating.'

'No,' disagrees the minister. 'He is obviously making a statement about the nature of God, the source of All Things Good. He is showing appreciation for the food by jumping for it... in a way it's a little like saying grace before eating.'

'You're both wrong,' says the scientist. 'He obviously created this table with advanced rules of thermodynamics in mind. Heat rises, therefore the heat in this room will rise to the ceiling, keeping the food on the table warmer for longer.' After some argument, the men finally ask why the man has such a tall dining table. 'Hmmm,' he says, 'Seems as I recall, I had a lot of wood and no saw to cut it with.'

★

Why is semen white and urine yellow?
So that men can tell if they're coming or going.

How are men and carpet alike?
If you lay them right the first time, you can walk all over them for years to come!

Confucius say... He who run behind bus get exhausted.

If at first you do succeed, try not to look too astonished.

Ever stop to think, and forget to start again?

A blonde stopped at a coke machine and put in a dollar. When a coke came out she put it on top of the machine. She then put another dollar in the machine and got another coke, and put it also on top. She did this about ten times, then a man behind her said, 'Do you mind if I put my dollar in and get one?' The blonde replied, 'Yes I do mind – can't you see, I'M WINNING!'

A blonde was coming home from work. As she turned into her street she noticed smoke coming out of her house. She started yelling, 'Fire! Fire! My place is on fire, come quick!' Then she called the fire brigade. She said, 'My house is on fire, my house is on fire, come quick.' The guy asked her how to get there and she said, 'In your big red truck, of course!'

Male Chauvinist Pigs!

How many male chauvinists does it take to change a light bulb in the kitchen?
Who cares? Let the bitch cook in the dark.

★

Why did the woman cross the road?
More to the point, what was she doing out of the kitchen?

★

Why do women have periods?
Because they deserve them.

What's the difference between a terrorist and a woman with PMS?
You can bargain with a terrorist.

What do you do when your washing-machine stops working?
Slap the bitch until she starts again.

The time had come. Aliens were going to blow up earth in five minutes. A group of friends were forlornly sharing a meal together, knowing it was the last time they would ever see each other. The only woman of the group suddenly said, 'Is there one last chance for me to be a real woman?' One of the blokes answered, 'Sure, love,' and taking off his shirt he said, 'Iron this.'

Why do men die before their wives?
They want to.

Why do men pass more gas than women?
Because women won't shut up long enough to build up pressure.

Bigamy is having one wife too many. Some say monogamy is the same.

★

One day an inquisitive little boy went to his mother and asked, 'Mummy, what's a pussy?' The mother took him out to the neighbour's house and showed her son their kitten. The next day the boy pulled on his mother's apron and asked, 'Mummy, what's a bitch?' The mother took him to the park, and walked around until she found a dog. 'There you go,' she said, pointing to it. 'This is a dog. A female dog is called a bitch.' The next day the boy sought confirmation from his father. 'Dad, what's a pussy?' His father knelt down beside the bed, pulled out an issue of Playboy and drew a circle around the middle section of one of the naked women. 'Son, that is a pussy.'
'Oh,' said the boy.
'What's a bitch then?'
'Everything outside of the circle,' replied his father.

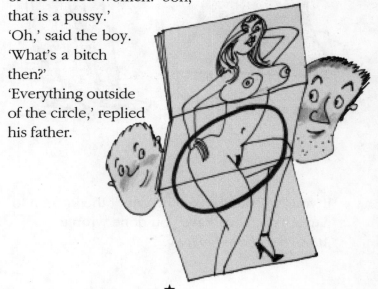

★

What do you say to a feminist that has no arms
or legs?
Nice tits.

★

If your wife keeps coming out of the kitchen to
nag at you, what have you done wrong?
Made her chain too long.

★

Why do cavemen drag their women by the hair?
Because if they dragged them by the feet, they would fill up with mud.

How can you tell if your wife is dead?
The sex is the same but the dishes keep piling up.

How do you turn a fox into an elephant?
Marry it!

Why do brides wear white?
Because that's the colour of all kitchen appliances!

WHY IS FRUIT SALAD BETTER THAN A WOMAN?

Fruit salad doesn't complain when you put whipped cream in it.

Fruit salad may be cold, but at least that's the way it's meant to be.

Fruit salad always looks good in the morning.

Fruit salad doesn't care if you fall asleep after eating it.

Fruit salad has soft *and* crunchy bits.

Fruit salad is cheaper.

— MALE CHAUVINIST PIGS! —

Your friends aren't interested in
stealing your fruit salad.

You can take fruit salad home to
your parents.

You can make fruit salad as sweet
as you want.

You can look at girly pictures while
having fruit salad.

You can put out a cigarette in a
bowl of fruit salad.

Fruit salad smells and tastes good.

Fruit salad goes down easier.

If you put icecream in your
fruit salad, it doesn't put on weight.

Fruit salad doesn't nag.

Fruit salad is ready in 15 minutes
or less.

You can't get a bowl of fruit salad
pregnant by putting cream in it.

Fruit salad doesn't have a time of the
month...it's good all the time.

When fruit salad gets too old, you
can compost it.

Fruit salad doesn't steal the doona.

Fruit salad doesn't mind if you wake up at 3 a.m. and decide to have some.

You can have an intelligent conversation with fruit salad.

No matter how ugly you are, you can always get a bowl of fruit salad.

What's the difference between a woman and a tornado?
Nothing. They both start with a blowjob and you end up losing your house.

How much do bachelors know about women anyway?
A lot. That's why they're still bachelors.

What do you call a man who's been lucky
in love?
A bachelor.

★

A man comes home from a hard day of work. After a relaxing dinner with his wife, they decide to have an early night. As the man lies in bed, his wife is brushing her teeth in the bathroom.

The man calls to his wife, 'My little boopey-boo, I'm lonely.'

So the woman comes out of the bathroom and crosses the room to the husband. On the way she trips on the carpet and falls on her face.

The husband, with a concerned look on his face says, 'Oh, did my little honey-woney fall on her little nosey-wosey?'

The woman picks herself up and gets into bed. The two have passionate sex and afterwards the woman gets up to go to the bathroom to clean up. On the way she catches her foot on the same bit of carpet and falls flat on her face.

The man looks at his wife lying on the floor and says, 'Clumsy bitch.'

Heaven, Hell and Other Biblical Stuff

One Saturday morning three men were standing in line at the Pearly Gates of Heaven. St Peter told the first man, 'I'm only admitting people in today who have had a really horrible death. How did you die?'

The first man replied, 'Well, I got home from work early one day and my wife was acting really strange, so I figured she was cheating on me. I could hear noises coming from somewhere but couldn't see anyone. I went outside and, sure enough, there was this bloke hanging off the balcony. I started bashing his fingers until he let go and fell. He landed in the bushes, still alive, so I rushed into the kitchen, grabbed the fridge and threw it at him. All of this caused a blood vessel in my brain to burst, killing me.'

'That sounds like a pretty bad death to me,' said St Peter as he let the man in. The second man then recounted his story. 'Every day I exercise on the balcony of my apartment. This morning as I was exercising I slipped and fell over the edge. Luckily I caught the railing of the balcony on the floor below me. But this maniac appears, and bashes my fingers until I have to let go. I get lucky again, and land in some bushes, not too badly hurt. Then, before I know it, a fridge falls out of the sky and crushes me to death.' Once again, St Peter conceded it was a horrible death. Then the third man told his story.

'Picture this,' he began. 'I'm lying naked inside a fridge...'

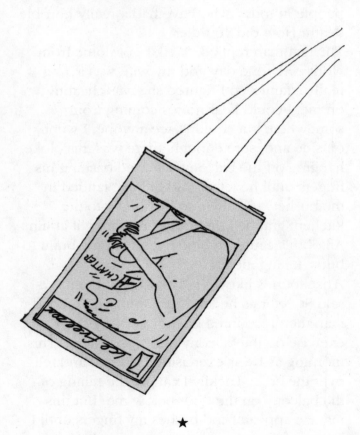

★

The two directors of a large business knew their office building was unsafe but were too stingy to make the necessary changes. As a result, the entire building burnt down to the ground, killing almost one hundred innocent people. Satan told the directors that they had two choices. They could spend the rest of eternity in the Cold Room, where their blood would freeze and their extremities would drop off, or they could spend it in the Hot Room, where their skin would blister and peel off slowly and painfully, layer after layer. Both choices sounded pretty bad to the directors. Suddenly one of them noticed the Sex Room, and with a huge smile he leapt toward it. Opening the door, he revealed a room full of directors getting blowjobs from the best looking secretaries he had ever seen. He turned to Satan and said with a wink, 'Hey, I think we want this room!' Satan shook his head and said, 'You can't go there...that's secretary Hell!'

A priest, a baptist minister and a rabbi in the same town all traded in their cars on nice new ones around the same time. Feeling the need to celebrate, the priest sprinkled water on his car's hood. Not to be outdone, the baptist minister drove his car into the lake. The rabbi thought for a while and then brought a hacksaw over to his car and carefully sawed off a half-inch of tailpipe.

★

In the beginning there was nothing, then God said 'Let there be light.'
And there was light. There was still nothing, but you could see it a lot better.

★

Jesus, hanging from the cross, sees Peter in the throng of people at the bottom of the hill. 'Peter!' he calls. Peter hears and says, 'I hear you, my Lord. I'm coming.' As he begins the climb a guard blocks his way and says, 'Stop, or I'll have to cut off your leg.' But Peter replies, 'I mustn't stop, my Lord is calling for me.' So he holds out his leg for the guard to cut off, then continues on, bleeding badly. Jesus continues to call, 'Peter, Peter!' Peter, in terrible pain, hops on up the hill, gasping, 'I'm coming, my Lord, I'm coming.' Just then he is stopped by another guard who says, 'I'll cut your arm off if you try to get past me,' so Peter holds his arm out and says, 'As you will. I must go to the Lord.' So the guard chops off his arm and Peter continues on, growing pale from the blood loss. Now crawling along up the hill, Peter hears Jesus calling again. 'I'll be there soon, my Lord!' promises Peter. Another guard blocks his way. 'Stop, or I will cut off your other arm,' said the guard. Weak and in pain, Peter holds out his arm to be chopped off. He says, 'Our Lord is beckoning me. I must go to him.' Now, armless and with only one leg, he somehow makes it to the top of the hill, dragging his bloody body to Jesus' feet. 'Lord, I have answered your call.' Jesus looks down at him and says, 'Hey guess what Peter! I can see your house from here!'

★

What do you call an Atheist Insomniac Dyslexic?
*Someone who stays up all night wondering if
there is a dog.*

There was a Pope who was loved by all men,
and when he died and went to heaven Saint
Peter met him with a warm embrace.
'Welcome your holiness, we are honoured to
have you here. Your dedication in serving your
fellow man has earned you great respect here,
and for this we grant you free access to all
parts of heaven. You may go anywhere and
speak to anyone. Now, is there anything which
your holiness desires?'
'Well, yes,' the Pope replied. 'I have spent
many years trying to work out the mysteries of
the Universe. I have spent hours pondering
questions that have confounded philosophers
through the ages. I would dearly love to read
any transcripts which recorded the actual con-
versations between God and the prophets of
old. I would love to see what was actually said,
first-hand.'
Saint Peter immediately ushered the Pope to
the heavenly library. The Pope sat down and
began to read the true history of the earth.
Some time later a scream of heart-chilling
anguish rang out from the bookshelves of the
library. Hordes of Angels came running. There

they found the Pope, with a look of complete
horror on his face, pointing to
a single word on an old,
old parchment, repeating
over and over, 'There's
an "R", there's an
"R" – it's
"celibRate!"'

★

Two nuns are bicycling down a cobblestone
street. The first one says to the other, 'I haven't
come this way before.' The second one says, 'I
know, it's the cobbles.'

★

How do you get a nun pregnant?
Dress her up as an altar boy.

★

An American called Jay arrived in Hell, and was told he had a choice to make. He could go to Capitalist Hell or to Communist Hell. Naturally, Jay wanted to compare the two, so he strolled on over to Capitalist Hell. There outside the door was a demon, looking bored. 'What's it like in there?' asked Jay. 'Well,' the demon replied, 'in Capitalist Hell, they cut your fingers off, boil you in oil, chain you to a tree, tear your kidneys out, then cut you up into small pieces with sharp knives.'

'That's terrible!' gasped Jay. 'I'm going to check out Communist Hell!' He wandered over to Communist Hell, where he discovered a huge line of people waiting to get in. Jay pushed his way through to the head of the line, where he asked one of the demons what Communist Hell was like. 'In Communist Hell,' the demon replied impatiently, 'they cut your fingers off, boil you in oil, chain you to a tree, tear your kidneys out, then cut you up into small pieces with sharp knives.'

'But ... but that's the same as Capitalist Hell!' protested Jay.

'True,' sighed the demon, 'but sometimes we don't have oil, sometimes we don't have knives ...'

★

A guy dies and goes to Hell. At the gates the Devil explains, 'You must choose one of the following rooms, and from this day forward, you will remain in that room for all eternity.' The Devil then takes him to the first room and opens the door. Inside, a circle of damned people with bowling balls strapped to their heads and feet walk around barefoot on hot coals. 'Oh, I don't think I want to live in this room,' says the man, so the Devil takes him to the second room. In this room, the damned are walking around on burning hot broken glass, listening to Mariah Carey. 'I don't think I could bear this room either,' says the man. So they walk on. In the last room, the damned are standing around up to their armpits in shit, drinking coffee. 'This doesn't look too bad!' says the man. 'I think I'll stay here for eternity.' 'Very well,' said the Devil, closing the door behind him. 'Hmm, nice coffee,' thinks the man, as a demon hands him a cup. Suddenly the room supervisor calls out on his megaphone, 'Okay everybody, coffee break's over! Back on your heads!'

★

A scruffy man wandered into a bar and sat down next to a priest. The man's clothes were dirty, he had lipstick smudges on his face, and a half-empty bottle of gin was sticking out of his pocket. He opened his newspaper and began listening to his headphones. After a few seconds he took the headphones off and turned to the priest. 'Hey, Father, what causes arthritis?'

The priest, eyeing the guy up and down in a disapproving manner, said, 'Arthritis is caused by loose living, running around with cheap, vulgar hussies, too much drink, and a contempt for fellow man.'

'Well I'll be damned,' muttered the drunk, putting his headphones back on. After a moment, the priest began to feel guilty about his unkind outburst. 'I'm very sorry, I was out of line. I really do apologise for my rudeness,' he said. 'How long have you had arthritis?'

'I don't have it, Father. I just heard here on the radio that the Pope does.'

Three guys die and are lined up at the Pearly Gates. St Peter asks them, 'Were you faithful to your wives?' The first guy answers, 'Yes. Never even thought about another woman.' St Peter says, 'Good man. See that Rolls Royce over there? That's yours to drive in Heaven.' The second guy says, 'Well, I had one short affair, but I confessed to my wife and we eventually sorted it out.' St Peter says, 'That was decent of you. Okay, see that small BMW over there? That's yours to drive around Heaven.' The third guy says, 'I hate to say this, but I cheated on my wife on our wedding night and continued doing so all my life.' St Peter says, 'That's okay. You can have that old Honda Civic over there.' The three guys get into their cars and start cruising around Heaven. A few weeks later, the second and third guys come across the first guy, sitting in his Rolls Royce and looking very depressed. 'Mate, what's wrong? You're driving a Rolls, you're in Heaven ... what's the matter with you? He says glumly, 'I saw my wife here yesterday.' The other two reply, 'But that's great! What's the problem?'

'She was driving a Datsun 120Y.'

★

Two men in black were both eating their lunch in a sunny park one day. After the normal small talk about the wonderful weather, one said to the other, 'So I assume you're a catholic priest?'

'That's right. And I guess you're a rabbi?'

'Yes, that's true.' The two munched on their sandwiches for a minute. After a while the rabbi leaned over and whispered, 'Have you ever broken a commandment?'

The priest nodded bashfully. 'I slept with a woman once.' He then said to the rabbi, 'Have you ever eaten pork?' The rabbi looked around to make sure no one passing by was listening.

'Yes,' he whispered. There was a short silence, which was broken by the priest.

'Sex is much better than pork isn't it!'

★

As Father Alan was aware that many of those in his parish were heavy drinkers he decided to preach a sermon to show that animals did not fall prey to the follies of alcohol as men did. He began the story of the peasant who travelled throughout the world with his trusty dog. One hot day, as a special treat, the peasant bought a bucket of beer for the dog, but the dog refused it. The peasant then gave the dog a bucket of water instead, which the dog drank thirstily. 'Tell me why the dog would drink the water and not the beer?' Father Alan asked. From the back of the church someone yelled, 'Because it was a bloody dog, that's why.'

For six years Father Frank had read sermons every Sunday morning at the small country church. Feeling it was time he moved on to a bigger church, Father Frank had taken up a position in a far away town. A morning tea party was held to say goodbye. Presenting him with a going-away present, one young woman said, 'We don't know what we will do without you Father. Until you came we didn't know what sin was.'

★

There was a priest and a choir boy who both wanted to study medicine at the local university. One day the choir boy went to take an entrance exam. He returned to the church the next day looking very down in the dumps. 'How was the exam?' asked his priest, hoping to get some tips, as his entrance exam was that afternoon. 'They asked quite a lot of "fill in the missing letter" questions about first aid and stuff. I got a score of 65%. It wasn't good enough to get in,' said the choir boy. The priest looked worried, but went to take the test anyway. The next day at church the choirboy asked the priest how the exam went. 'I went very badly. I think I got all wrong but one.'
'Which question was that?'
'It was... "What do you do when you come across an unconscious lady? You feel her pu_s_?"'
'Yeah, that's easy,' said the boy. 'The answer is "pulse".'
'Damn,' said the priest. 'Got that one wrong too.'

★

As it was such a nice day, the vicar called the church to say he was too sick to take morning service that Sunday. He loaded up his fishing gear and went down to the beach. God, watching from up above, didn't think the bishop should get away with this. He called one of the angels over to watch what he was going to do. The vicar cast his line and immediately caught a 100 kg fish, the biggest he had ever seen in his entire life, let alone caught.

'I thought you were going to punish him,' said the angel, disappointed.

'I have,' replied God. 'Who is he going to tell?'

★

A man accidentally falls over a cliff, and in the panicked moments on the way down he manages to grab onto the only branch within reach or sight. In a few moments he summons enough strength to move again, and he yells, 'Help! Is there anyone up there who can help me?'

A moment passes without event, and he again cries, 'Help! Can anyone hear me? I need help!' After another moment a booming voice answers, 'This is the voice of God. Believe in me. Have faith. Say a prayer and let go of the branch. You will float gently to the ground, unharmed. Just let go.'

Looking down at the jagged rocks and the pounding surf, the man thinks for a second, and then calls up, 'Is there anyone ELSE up there?'

★

A faith healer is addressing his audience, convincing them of the benefits of faith and prayer as a means of curing the sick. He asks for volunteers from the audience so that he can demonstrate his powers. Two young men come forward.

'What ails you, lad?' says the healer to the first man, named Robbie.

'I h-have a b-b-bad s-s-s-stammer,' is the reply.

'And you?' the healer says to Ken, the second man, who leans unsteadily on wooden crutches.

'I've been a partial cripple since birth.'

'Now,' says the healer, 'I will show you how the power of our Lord will help you overcome your illness.' He lays one hand across Robbie's mouth, and the other on Ken's leg, and encourages his audience to pray together. He whips everyone into such a frenzy that they all believe that anything is possible, then he says to the two men, 'Do you have faith in God, do you believe in the power?'

'YES!' says Ken.

'Y-Y-YES,' says Robbie.

'Now I want you to go behind that screen and do exactly as I say.' So Ken and Robbie go behind the screen and the healer says, 'Ken, if you truly believe then throw out your crutches,' and, to everyone's amazement, Ken's crutches come sailing over the top of the screen. Then the healer says, 'Now Robbie, if you truly believe, say something!' and after a hushed silence, a voice rings out, 'K-k-k-ken's f-f-fallen over.'

What's the definition of a masochist?
A celibate priest. They give up their sex lives, only to have people come in and tell them the highlights.

One Tuesday morning a guy arrives at the pearly gates. He waits there for ages until he has reached the front of the queue. St Peter is leafing through the Big Book to see if the guy is worthy of entering Heaven. After several minutes, St Peter closes the book, furrows his brow, and says, 'You haven't done anything really spectacularly good in your life, but you also haven't done anything bad. Tell you what, if you can tell me one really good deed that you did in your life, I'll let you in.'

The guy thinks for a moment and says, 'Okay, well there was this one time when I was out driving and I saw a gang assaulting this poor girl. There were about 20 of them. So I slowed down, got out of my car, grabbed the jack out of the boot, and walked straight up to the leader of the gang. He was a huge guy with a studded leather jacket and a chain running from his nose to his ear. As I walked up to the leader, the gang members formed a circle around me. So, I ripped the leader's chain out of his face and smashed him over the head with the jack,' the guy says. Then I turned around and yelled at the rest of them, "Leave this poor, innocent girl alone! You're all a bunch of sick, deranged animals! Go home before I kill the lot of you!"'

St Peter, very impressed, says, 'Wow! When did this happen?'

'About ten minutes ago.'

★

An Amish boy and his father were in a shopping centre. They were amazed by almost everything they saw, but especially by two shiny, silver walls that could move apart and back together again. The boy asked his father, 'What is this, Father?' The father responded, 'Son, I have never seen anything like this in my life. I don't know what it is.' While the boy and his father were watching wide-eyed an old lady in a wheelchair rolled up to the moving walls and pressed a button. The walls opened and the lady rolled between them into a small room. The walls closed and the boy and his father watched small circles of lights with numbers above the walls light up. They continued to watch as the circles began to light up in the reverse direction. The walls opened up again and a beautiful young woman stepped out, smiling seductively. The father turned to his son and said, 'Quick... go get your mother.'

★

It's a sunny day, and a priest decides to take a walk to the pier. He greets a fisherman along the way and the two begin talking. The fisherman asks if the priest has ever fished before, to which the priest answers no. So the fisherman says, 'Well, give this a go, Father.' And what do you know, the priest immediately catches a big one, a huge one in fact.

'Wow, look at that sonofabitch!' exclaims the fisherman in admiration.

Priest: 'Uh, sir, can you please mind your language?'

Fisherman: (a quick thinker, this one) 'I do apologise, Father, but that's what the fish is called: a sonofabitch.'

Priest: 'Oh, I'm sorry, I'm not normally a seafood eater, I am not aware of the terminology.'

After the trip, the priest takes his prize catch to the Bishop.

Priest: 'Look at this big sonofabitch!'

Bishop (shocked)*:* 'Please, mind your language, we are in church!'

Priest: 'No, it's alright! That's what the fish is called and I caught it. I caught this sonofabitch!'

Bishop: 'Oh. Well, I could clean this sonofabitch and have it for dinner.'

So the bishop takes the fish, cleans it and takes it to the Head Mother.

Bishop: 'Could you cook this sonofabitch for dinner tonight?'

Head Mother: 'Goodness, what language!'

Bishop: 'No, that's what this fish is called, a sonofabitch! Father caught it, I cleaned it, and we want you to cook it.'

Head Mother: 'Oh okay, I'll cook the sonofabitch tonight.'

That night the Pope stops by for dinner. He thinks the fish is great and asks where they got it.

Priest: 'I caught the sonofabitch.'

Bishop: 'And I cleaned the sonofabitch.'

Head Mother: 'And I cooked the sonofabitch.'

The Pope stares at them for a minute with a steely gaze, pours a whisky, pops a cigar into his mouth, puts his feet up on the table and says, 'You know, you bloody motherf***ers are alright!'

★

'Okay, listen!' commanded Noah. 'On my ark there will be absolutely no sex. No kissing, no fondling, no nothing. Now, all you males, take off your dicks and hand them to my sons. I'll give you a receipt for your dick, and once we see land I'll give your dicks back to you.'

After a few days Mr Rabbit hopped into his wife's cage. 'Quick!' he said in excitement. 'Get on my shoulders and look out the window to see if there is any land there yet!'

Mrs Rabbit got onto his shoulders and looked out at the ocean.

'Nope,' she said. 'No land yet.'

'Shit!' yelled Mr Rabbit. This went on every day until Mrs Rabbit got fed up with him. 'What is the matter with you? You know it will rain for forty days and nights. Only after the water has drained will we be able to see land. Why are you acting so excited all the time?'

'Look!' said Mr Rabbit with a crazy, joyous look on his face as he held out a piece of paper. 'I GOT THE DONKEY'S RECEIPT!!'

★

A couple of politicians, very much in love, were both killed in a car crash. When they got to Heaven they wanted to continue practising politics so they requested an election. They drew up election speeches and worked out policies, but it took St Peter an awfully long time to find another politician to run against them in the election. After a long struggle, they became the winning candidates, and decided they performed so well together as a political entity that they should also get married. So they trundled off to St Peter to ask him to supply a priest to perform the wedding ceremony. 'Are you kidding?' said St Peter. 'It took me 100 years to find another politician in Heaven to run against you in the election. I'll never be able to find a priest in Heaven to marry you!'

There was a man who had terminal cancer and only had ten days left to live. He told his family to sell all he had and trade in his money for gold and bury it with him in a suitcase, as he wanted to take it to the next world. After he had passed away, he approached St Peter at the pearly gates. When St Peter asked him to explain what he was doing with a suitcase, the man replied, 'I brought the most important thing to me in the world, the most valuable possession I have.'
Curious, St Peter asked what it was. The man excitedly opened his suitcase for him to see, and upon viewing the gold inside, St Peter drew a perplexed face and asked, 'Pavement?'

★

Three priests, all travelling by train into the city for a religious convention, happened to be sitting in the same carriage. Becoming familiar with one another, they began to confess their sins. 'I can't resist women,' said the first priest. 'I have succumbed to temptation time and time again.'

'I can't keep off the booze,' said the second. 'At least once a week I end up lying naked in a drunken stupor on the dining table.' The third priest was quiet.

'So what's your vice?' asked the first priest. 'Gambling, stealing from the collection plate?'

'No,' replied the third priest. 'My sin is a bad one. I gossip, and I can hardly wait to get to that convention.'

★

An elderly vicar visited a farm in the country one day to sell his horse. A farmer for years, Bluey knew a good horse when he saw one and agreed to buy it. But when Bluey jumped on the horse, rearing to go, it would not move an inch. 'Oh, sorry,' said the vicar. 'The horse is religious. He'll only go when you say "Jesus Christ", and will only stop when you say "Amen".' Bluey thanked the vicar, said 'Jesus Christ,' and was off sprinting around the countryside. After riding for only an hour they suddenly found themselves in a shooting range. BANG! A gun fired right next to them, sending the horse into a galloping frenzy. As Bluey was taken at full bolt through the bush he closed his eyes, trying desperately to think of the word to make it stop, finally yelling, 'Amen!' The horse skidded to a halt and when Bluey's heart had stopped racing he opened up his eyes and saw that they had stopped right on the edge of a terrifying mountain chasm. 'Jesus Christ,' he said.

★

What's a catch-22 situation for a Jew?
Free pork!

★

Two very devout Catholics, who had been
dating for several years, were out driving in a
desolate area in the country one day when
their car broke down. As the only mechanic
within 100 miles of the town was busy with
another job, the two decided they would have
to spend the night at a motel. There was only
one motel within walking distance, and there
was only one room available, with only one
bed. 'Well,' said the boyfriend to the girlfriend,
'it looks like we are going to have to sleep in
the same room tonight. I don't think the Good

Lord or our parents will mind if we share the same bed, just this once.'

'Okay,' replied the girlfriend. They got ready for bed, and each took their agreed place at either extreme of the bed. Ten minutes later the girlfriend said, 'I'm really cold.'

'Okay, I'll get you a blanket,' said the boyfriend, and he got out of bed and found a blanket in the cupboard. Ten minutes later the girlfriend said, 'I'm still really, really cold.'

'Okay, then, I'll get you another blanket,' said the boyfriend, getting up once more to fetch a blanket from the closet. Ten minutes later the girlfriend said, 'Look, I'm still freezing. I don't think the Lord would mind if we acted as man and wife for just this one night.'

'You're probably right,' said the boyfriend. 'Get up and get your own damn blanket.'

A priest decides it's time to pay a visit to a nearby convent that is in an undesirable part of town. As he looks for the convent he is approached by several prostitutes who proposition him. 'Thirty bucks a trick!' Not knowing exactly what this meant, the embarrassed priest hurries on to the convent. Inside he asks Mother Superior, 'What's a trick?' She answers, 'Thirty bucks, just like out on the street!'

★

A man was caught in a flash flood and had only a thin tree branch to hang onto to prevent him from being washed into the water. As the water became stronger and he began to tire, a motorboat appeared out of nowhere.

'Come on mate, get in,' yelled the boatman.

'It's okay,' the man said. 'I have faith in Jesus. He will save me.' So the boat continued on and the water began to rise. When it was up to his neck another boat appeared. 'Better get in or you'll drown,' shouted the boatman.

'No, it's okay,' said the man. 'I have faith in Jesus. He will save me.' The boatman shrugged and rowed away. By this time the water had reached the man's chin. A third boat appeared. 'This is your last chance, get in!' yelled the boatman. 'No, Jesus will save me.' The boat went off and seconds later, the man drowned. Arriving in Heaven he was greeted by Jesus. 'Hey, Jesus, I trusted in you and you let me drown! I don't believe it!'

'Neither do I. I sent three f***ing boats to save you.'

★

'You're not a hypnotist, are you?' asked the doorman of the jazz club. 'No, I'm a singer,' the bloke replied. 'Come right this way then,' said the doorman, taking the singer to see the Manager. 'You better not tell me you're a hypnotist!' said the Manager grimly.

'No! I'm a singer,' said the bloke. The Manager took the bloke over to Madeleine, the pianist. They began to rehearse and at the end of the first song Madeleine asked, slightly worried, 'You're not going to do anything else in your act are you? No hypnotism or anything?' The singer shook his head in frustration. 'Look, I keep telling everyone I'm a singer. What's all this crap about hypnotism?'

'Well,' said Madeleine. 'Last week we hosted a convention for priests and nuns. We thought we'd better not hire a comedian because, well, you know what innocent folk those of the calling are. So we brought in a hypnotist instead. The convention filled the whole audience – that's over 200 people! The hypnotist was pretty damn good, too, got them all in a trance!'

'Well, so what was the problem?'

'Well,' said Madeleine, 'Halfway through the act he slipped on something on the floor and went arse over tit off the stage. Landed on his nose and broke it, yelled, "F***!" You can just imagine what God's thinking of us now!'

★

One day Jesus comes across an angry, stone-clenching, mob encircling a screaming woman. 'What's going on?' he demands. 'She's an adulteress,' cries a voice. 'She must be stoned to death.'

'Let he who is without sin cast the first stone,' replies Jesus, staring back at the crowd. At this, they fall silent, then one by one they drop their stones and shuffle off, ashamed. Except for one little old woman who staggers up to the adulteress with a monster of a rock in her arms. She raises it above her head and smashes it down on the other woman, killing her instantly. Jesus lets out a huge sigh then says, 'You know, Mum, sometimes you really piss me off.'

★

A Jewish man meets his non-Jewish friend one Friday for lunch.

Non-Jew: 'So, you can't eat shellfish, anything with a split hoof or any animal that chews its cud?'

Jew: 'Right.'

Non-Jew: 'Well, what if a horse's hooves were magically unsplit? Could you eat a horse then?'

Jew: 'Hmm, I guess so.'

Non-Jew: 'You mean you could eat a WHOLE horse?'

★

Early one morning a nun is walking through the city. She sees a drunk lying in the gutter outside a pub with his head resting on an empty beer bottle. She stops and says to him, 'You poor man. Don't you know that alcohol will ruin your life? Come to the catholic mission with me and I'll help you stop drinking.'

The drunk opens one eye, looks up and says, 'Sister, you don't know what you're talking about. A little drink now and then won't hurt anyone. But if you come inside and have a drink I will go with you to your mission.'

The nun thinks it was worth doing in order to get him to the mission so she agrees, but she says, 'Can you bring it out here? I don't want to be seen drinking in a bar.'

'Sure, no problem,' says the drunk.

'Oh, and another thing,' says the nun. 'Can you put my drink in a coffee mug?'

'Okay,' agrees the drunk, and he goes into the pub and says to the bartender, 'A double bourbon, and put it in a coffee mug!'

The bartender says, 'What, is that nun out there again?'

★

Turn On the Lights!

How many men does it take to change a light bulb?
Four. One to actually change it, and three friends to brag to about how he screwed it.

How many real men does it take to change a light bulb?
None. Real men aren't afraid of the dark.

How many feminists does it take to change a light bulb?
Five, one to screw it in and four to host a women-only seminar on how the bulb is exploiting the socket.

How many council workers does it take to change a light bulb?
You're kidding aren't you?

How many Miss Americas does it take to change a light bulb?
Just one. She holds the bulb and the world revolves around her.

★

How many hippies does it take to change a light bulb?
Six. One to screw it in, and five to share the experience.

How many civil libertarians does it take to change a light bulb?
None. If you want to sit in the dark, that's your business.

How many social workers does it take to change a light bulb?
Only one. But the light bulb has to want to change.

How many cafeteria staff does it take to change a light bulb?
Sorry, we closed 12 seconds ago and I've already counted the till.

How many politicians does it take to change a light bulb?
Two. One to screw it in and one to screw it up.

How many fishermen does it take to change a light bulb?
One. And you should have seen it! It was this big!

How many pro-lifers does it take to change a light bulb?
Five. Two to screw in the bulb, two to testify that it was lit from the moment they began screwing, and one to shoot them all, just in case they are pro-choice.

How many psychotherapists does it take to change a light bulb?
Just one, but it takes 30 visits at $90 a session.

How many mechanics does it take to change a light bulb?
Five. One to force it with a hammer, one to tell you it's no longer in warranty, and three to go out for more bulbs.

How many PhD students does it take to change a light bulb?
'You'll find out when I present my thesis on it in five years.'

How many actors does it take to change a light bulb?

Ten. One to climb the ladder, and nine to stand around grumbling, 'That should be me up there.'

★

How many models does it take to change a
light bulb?
*A whole room full, but they're all too busy
doing their hair.*

How many actresses does it take to change a
light bulb?
*One. But you should have seen the line outside
the producer's hotel room.*

How many movie directors does it take to
change a light bulb?
*Just one, and when it's finished, everyone
thinks that his first light bulb was much better.*

How many women with PMS does it take to
change a light bulb?
Three. Why three? It just does, that's why.

How many scriptwriters does it take to change
a light bulb?
Why do we have to change it?

★

How many art gallery visitors does it take to
change a light bulb?
*Two – one to do it and the other to say any
four year old could do it better.*

— TURN ON THE LIGHTS! —

How many technical writers does it take to change a light bulb?
Just one, provided there is a programmer around to explain how to do it.

How many actresses does it take to change a light bulb?
Just one. They don't like sharing the spotlight.

How many Microsoft executives does it take to screw in a light bulb?
None. They just redefine 'darkness' as the industry standard.

How many sound men does it take to change a light bulb?
One two three. One two three...

How many mystery writers does it take to
change a light bulb?
*Two. One to screw it in almost all the way and
another to give it a surprise twist at the end.*

★

Politicians and Other Crooks

How long does it take for a female politician to have a shit?
Nine months.

★

A scientist, a salesman and a politician are driving along the countryside, and decide to spend the night in a small inn. 'I only have two free beds, so one of you will have to sleep in the barn,' says the innkeeper. The scientist volunteers to do so and makes his way out to the yard. A short time later, when the others have settled into their beds, the scientist knocks on the door. 'There's a cow in the barn. I'm Hindu and it is against my religion to sleep next to a sacred animal.' So the salesman says, 'Okay, I'll sleep out there then.' He gathers up his blankets and heads to the shed. A few seconds later he is back, saying, 'There's a pig in the barn. I'm Jewish and it would offend me to sleep next to an unclean animal.' So the politician is sent to the barn. A minute later there is knocking again, only this time much louder. The scientist and salesman open the door and see that it's the cow and the pig.

A sign outside the Free Range Lion Safari Park: Adults, $10. Children $5. Politicians, free.

If a politician or a tax inspector were both
about to be burnt to death in a fire, and you
could only save one of them, would you make
a cup of coffee or take a nap?

What do you call a cross between a politician
and a boomerang?
A nasty smell you can't get rid of.

What do you do if you run over a politician?
Reverse.

What's the difference between a dead dog in
the road and a dead politician in the road?
Skid marks in front of the dog.

How do you stop a politician from drowning?
Take your foot off his head!

What's black and brown and looks good on a politician?
A doberman.

What do you have when a lawyer is buried up to his neck in sand?
Not enough sand.

Father Christmas, the Tooth Fairy, a smart blonde, an honest politician and a homeless old man are walking down the street together when they simultaneously spot a $50 note. Who gets it? The homeless old man, of course. The other four are mythological creatures.

★

A customer goes into a brain store.
'How much for engineer brain?'
'$3 a kilo.'
'How much for doctor brain?'
'$5 a kilo.'
'How much for politician brain?'
'$500 a kilo.'
'Why is politician brain so much more expensive?'
'Do you know how many politicians you need to kill to get a kilo of brain?'

In a biological science tutorial, one student commented to another, 'Hey, did you know that in our lab we're using politicians now instead of rats?'
'Really?' the other replied. 'How come?'
'Well, for three reasons: first, there are more politicians in alleys and back streets than rats; second, the lab assistants don't get attached to them; and third, there are some things that even a rat won't do. The only problem with using politicians however is that it's far more difficult to apply our findings to real human beings.'

What happens to a politician who takes Viagra?
He grows taller.

Lord, give me the ability to accept the things I cannot change, the strength of will to change the things that need changing, and the wisdom to hide the bodies of those people I had to kill because they pissed me off.

Why did the post office have to recall the new 'politician' stamps?
Because people couldn't tell which side to spit on.

A politician and a librarian were holidaying in an expensive resort in Fiji. The politician said, 'I'm here with my insurance money, because my house burnt down and everything I owned was destroyed by fire.'
'That's a bit of a coincidence,' said the librarian. 'I'm here because my house and all my belongings were destroyed by flood, and my insurance also paid for everything.'
The politician looked puzzled. 'How do you start a flood?'

A politician was approached by the Devil, who promised him that he could arrange it so that the politician would win every election and be ruler of the world before he turned 50. All he had to do was sell his soul, his wife's soul, his child's soul, and the souls of all his ancestors. The politician looked puzzled for a minute and asked, 'So what's the catch?'

★

Why won't snakes attack politicians?
Professional loyalty.

★

The homework assignment for Grade 3 required each child to draw a picture of their parents, showing what they did for a living. The teacher looked at everyone's homework the next day in class. 'Josh, that's a nice picture of a laboratory. Is your mother a scientist?' asked the teacher.

'Yes,' he answered proudly. 'Claire, I'm guessing from your picture of sausages that your daddy is a butcher.'

'Yes, he is,' replied Claire. But the teacher looked puzzled when she came to Benny's picture of a house, decorated with red fairy lights.

'Benny, that's a nice picture, but what exactly does your dad do?'

Benny announced, 'My dad's a pimp in a whore house.' The teacher was shocked, and promptly changed the subject. That night she phoned Benny's father. She told him about Benny's picture and demanded an explanation. Benny's father said, 'Well, actually, I'm a politician, but how do I explain a thing like that to an eight year old?'

★

Why do they always bury politicians 12 feet deep?
Because deep down, politicians are okay.

★

It's a lovely day, and a woman is sitting on a park bench, enjoying the sunshine, when a man comes along and sits down right beside her. Ripping open a bag of fresh prawns, he rips the shells off and throws them in the grass. After he has done this several times the woman says, 'Please don't do that. It's a disgusting sight and you're littering the park.'

The man replies, 'Listen, you. This is a private park, and I'll do what I bloody want.' And he continues to eat his prawns and throw the shells on the grass. Eventually he finishes them and shuts his eyes to have a bit of a nap in the sunshine. The woman then starts knitting.

Click, click, click. All the man can hear while he is trying to sleep is the incessant clicking of the needles. After about 15 minutes he opens one eye and says to the woman, 'Can you stop that noise – can't you see I'm trying to have a rest?'

'It's a public park and I can do what I like!' replies the woman smugly. At that, the man grabs the woman's knitting and throws it in the bin. The woman screams for the police. The man says, 'You know, you'll be fined $200 for wasting the cops' time.'

The woman replies, 'Well, you know, you'll get six years when the police smell your fingers!'

★

The Mafia newsletter began a Letters to the Editor column in which Mafia members were invited to freely express any grievance or political opinion they cared to. The only stipulation was that letters were to be signed with name, address and next of kin.

Join the Army, meet interesting people, kill them.

It's easy to distinguish the Mafia from the musicians. The musicians are the ones without the violin cases.

What's the ideal weight for a lawyer?
About two kilos, including the urn.

Judge:	'Did you stab the victim to death?'
Defendant:	'No I didn't.'
Judge:	'Do you realise what the penalties are for perjury?'
Defendant:	'Yes, and they're a damn lot better than the penalty for murder.'

★

The Italian crookster was returning to Rome. He had arranged two appointments; the first with the Pope, the second with the Mafia boss. 'Who should I see first?' He asked his adviser. 'The Pope,' was the response. 'You've only got to kiss his hand.'

★

Staking out a notoriously bad street for drunk drivers, a policeman watched from his car as a guy lurched through a pub door, tripped on the curb and stumbled into a car, falling asleep on the front seat. One by one, the drivers of the other cars drove off. Finally, the sleeper woke up, started his car and began to leave. The cop pulled him over and administered a breathalyser test. When the results showed a 0.0 blood-alcohol level, the puzzled policeman asked him how that was possible. 'Easy,' came the reply. 'Tonight was my turn to be the decoy.'

★

The Federal Bureau of Intelligence was hiring new recruits. Three men were called in for an interview. The interviewer, a thick-set, nasty looking man, told the first of the interviewees, 'One of the selection criteria for this position is undying loyalty to this organisation. We expect you to do everything you are told, no questions asked. We want you to take this gun, go into the other room and shoot your wife.' The first interviewee refused. 'Sorry, it's against my principles to do that.' He was promptly asked to leave and never again apply for a position there. The second applicant was then called in and given the same instruction. 'I can't do that,' he protested. 'It's our tenth anniversary tomorrow.' The interviewer thanked him for his time, but told him to leave and never again apply for a position there. The last interviewee was then shown in, and given the same instruction. 'Okay, no problem, I'll go do it now.' And he went into the other room where his wife was waiting. Shots were fired. Then all sorts of noises were heard ... grunting and groaning, a shriek here and there, a thud or two. Finally the third applicant returned and was asked what had happened. He replied, 'Some reject put blanks in the gun. So I had to strangle her.'

★

The three bears returned home from an early morning walk to find the door of their house wide open. Cautiously they went inside. 'Someone's been eating my porridge,' Papa Bear said. 'And someone's been eating my porridge,' Mama Bear said. Baby Bear rushed in. 'Bugger the porridge. Someone's nicked the video.'

One day a man is at a casino playing the one-arm bandits when he notices a frog sitting next to him. 'Ribbit,' says the frog, 'use this machine.' A little weirded out, the man nevertheless swaps machines, and what do you know, his first go and he lands the jackpot. 'Crikey!' he thinks. The frog then says, 'Ribbit, now use that machine over there.' So the man goes over to the machine and sits down, and straight away the coins are pouring out all over him. 'I'm on a really good thing here,' he thinks to himself, and decides to take the frog to Las Vegas where the big money is at. So that night the man and the frog board a plane and arrive there the following day.

After playing the tables for only ten minutes the man is a millionaire, thanks entirely to the frog and his strange lucky ways.

He says, 'Frog, I don't know how to repay you.

What can I do to show my appreciation?'
The frog replies, 'Ribbit, ribbit, kiss me.' The
man figures, well, why not, if that would make
the frog happy, so be it. So he bends down
and gives the frog a big sloppy kiss and the
frog magically turns in to a gorgeous 15 year
old girl.

'And that, your honour, is how the girl ended
up in my room.'

★

A police officer pulls over this guy who had
been weaving in and out of the lanes. He
goes up to the guy's window and says, 'Sir,
I need you to blow into this breathalyser tube.'
The man says, 'Sorry officer, I can't do that. I
am an asthmatic. If I do that I'll have a really
bad asthma attack.'

'Okay, fine. I need you to come down to the
station to give a blood sample.'

'I can't do that either. I am a haemophiliac. If I
do that, I'll bleed to death.'

'Well, then we need a urine sample.'

'I'm sorry, officer, no can do. I'm also a
diabetic. If I do that I'll get really low blood
sugar.'

'Okay then I need you to come out here
and walk this white line.'

'I can't do that, officer.'

'Why not?'

'Because I'm drunk.'

★

Irishmen and Other Funny Buggers...

A Russian, an American and an Israeli are waiting to order in a restaurant. The waiter says, 'Excuse me, but I've got bad news. There's a shortage of meat.'
The American asks, 'What's a shortage?'
The Russian asks, 'What's meat?'
The Israeli asks, 'What's excuse me?'

A rich American, touring the outback, stopped for lunch in a one-horse town.
After eating a ham sandwich, he was presented with a bill for $40. 'My God!' he exclaimed. 'Is ham that rare out here?'
'Nope,' said the owner. 'But rich Yanks are.'

The Russian woman went into the shop and said to the shopkeeper, 'Don't you have any bread?' The shopkeeper replies, 'Oh, you've got the wrong store. The shop next door is the bread shop and they have no bread. This is the milk bar, and we have no milk.'

Polva was in Moscow doing her weekly shopping. She went to the bakery, but as there was such a long queue she decided to walk on. The queue at the butcher store was even longer so instead she tried the grocery store, where the queue was longer than the bakery and butcher queues put together. 'I've had enough of this,' she said in frustration. Grabbing her husband's gun, she decided to march down to the Kremlin and do away with the Secretary General. But when she got there she found 200 people in line before her.

★

A couple from Tasmania were honeymooning
in a hotel. As they got into bed, the wife
looked over to her new husband and said,
'I've never done this before – please be gen-
tle.' A scared look instantly appeared on the
husband's face and he leapt out of bed and to
the phone. 'Dad, she's a virgin, what do I do?'
'Come home, son. If she's not good enough
for her family, she's not good enough for ours.'

An Irishman and a Scottish lass were having
sex. 'Cor, that wasn't very good,' remarked the
Scot. 'Aren't Irish men supposed to be thick?'
'Aren't Scots supposed to be tight?'

Why do New Zealand horses run so fast?
*Because they've seen what New Zealanders do
to the sheep.*

★

Why did the New Zealander invent velcro?
*Because the sheep started to recognise the
sound of a zip.*

★

The Japanese tourist gave a traveller's cheque
to the bank teller. When he counted his money
he said, 'Why do I get less money today?'
'Fluctuations,' said the teller.
'And fluck you lot too,' said the tourist.

★

Two Irish hunters were driving through the
country to go bear hunting. They came upon a
fork in the road where a sign read 'BEAR LEFT'
so they went home.

★

A couple of English lads were buying some
groceries at the supermarket when a
Catholic priest, wearing his left arm in a sling,
asked them to reach up and get him down
some dishwashing detergent from the top shelf.
'What happened to your arm?' asked one of
the lads.
'Oh, I broke it. I slipped as I was getting out of
the bath.' There was a silence until the priest
disappeared into the next aisle.
'What's a bath?' said one lad to the other.
'I dunno,' he replied. 'I'm not Catholic.'

An Irishman had been chugging down whisky
all night when the bartender called out, 'Okay,
people, bar's closing.' So the Irishman slurped
down the last of his drink, stood up to leave
and fell flat on his face. He tried to stand one
more time; same result. He figured he'd crawl
outside – hopefully the fresh air would sober
him up. Once outside he stood up and fell flat
on his face again. So he began to crawl home.
When he finally arrived at the door he stood
up and again fell flat on his face. He crawled
through the door and into his bedroom. When
he reached his bed he tried one more time to
stand up. This time he managed to pull himself
upright, but he quickly fell right into bed and

was sound asleep as soon as his head hit the pillow. The next morning his wife prodded him awake and said, 'So, you've been out drinking again, huh?'

'What makes you say that?' he asked, putting on an innocent look.

'The pub called – you left your wheelchair there again.'

★

What was written on the walls of an English brothel?

Please tell the girls when you're finished.

★

An Irish couple were cleaning out their garage when the husband accidently kicked over a bottle and broke it. Instantly a genie appeared, and said to them both, 'Thank you so much for freeing me from that ghastly bottle. To show my gratitude, I will grant you two wishes. The third I will keep for myself.'

The husband asked for a promotion at work, and the wife asked for a multi-million dollar annual salary. The genie obliged.

'Now for my wish,' began the genie. 'I wish to have my way with your wife. After all, I've made you successful,' he said to the husband, 'and you rich,' he said to the woman.

The husband and wife agreed that this was fair enough, and she went off to the bedroom with the genie, whereupon he proceeded to have his way with her. After they had finished doing the deed, the genie asked the wife if she would mind if he asked her a few questions.

'No, I don't mind,' she said.

'How long have you been married?'

She replied, 'Six years.'

The genie then asked, 'How old is your husband?'

To which she answered, '36'.

Then the genie asked, 'So, how long has he believed in this genie stuff?'

★

An Irish couple went to the family planning clinic. 'We've been married for over ten years and still have no children. Our friends think it's because we're stupid.'

'Rubbish,' said the doctor. 'It's most likely to do with the timing. How often do you do it?'

'Do what?' asked the wife.

★

An Italian boy and a Jewish boy come of age at the same time. The Italian boy's father presents him with a brand new pistol. On the other side of town, at his Bar Mitzvah, the Jewish boy receives a beautiful gold watch. The next day when the two boys see each other at school they show each other what they got. It turns out that each boy likes the other's present better, and so they trade. That night, when the Italian boy is at home, his father sees him looking at the watch.

'Where did you getta thatta watch?' asks the father. The boy explains that he and his Jewish friend had traded. The father blows his top. 'Whatta you? Stupidda boy? Whatsa matta you? Somma day, you maybe gonna getta married. Then maybe somma day you gonna comma home and finda you wife inna bed with another man. Whatta you gonna do then? Looka atta you watch and say, "How longa you gonna be?"'

Sick, Dirty, and Downright Disgusting

What's the difference between snot
and brussel sprouts?
You can't get a kid to eat brussel sprouts.

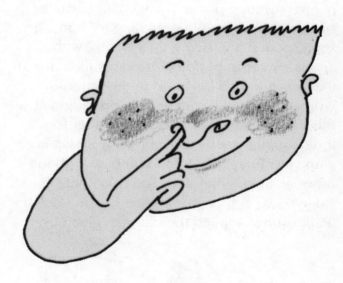

★

An old man and old woman met in a retirement home. After dating for a month, the old man said to the woman, 'I know we're old and can't do much sexually anymore. But if I pulled out my penis, would you hold it?' The woman obliged, so every day for the next two months the couple would sit in the park by the lake and the old woman would hold the man's penis. One day the man didn't show up at their regular meeting place. The woman became concerned and set out searching for him. She soon spotted him sitting on a bench, with another woman beside him. She walked up to the bench to find his penis in the other woman's hand. She felt terribly distraught at this and sobbed, 'We've been together for three months now. I thought we were getting along just fine. Now I find you here with this other woman. What does she have that I don't?'

'Parkinson's!' replied the old man gleefully.

★

Out on the bowling green one day, a man finds a lamp. He rubs the lamp, and a genie appears to grant him one wish. The bowler does not hesitate to think – he says, 'I'd like to be the best lawn bowler in my club.'

'No problem,' says the genie, 'but your sex life will be reduced as a side effect.' The genie blinks twice, and the deed is done. A few months later the genie reappears and asks the man how his bowling is going. 'Great,' says the man. 'I'm now the best in the club.'

'And how's your sex life now?'

'It's okay. I'm still getting a bit a few times a month.'

'Is that all?' exclaimed the genie.

'Well,' says the bowler. 'I don't think it's too bad for an aging scout leader with a very small troop.'

★

A man goes into a bar, takes a seat and says, 'Rum and coke, thanks.' The bartender goes over to the fruit bowl and places an apple in front of the man. 'Take a bite,' he says. The man takes a bite and miraculously, it takes like rum. The bartender smiles and says, 'Now turn it around.' He does and it tastes like coke. A little later the same man says, 'Gimme a vodka and orange.' The bartender once again places an apple in front of him. The man takes a bite, and what do you know, it tastes like vodka. 'Turn it around,' says the bartender. The man turns the apple around and takes another bite, and you guessed it, it tastes like orange. Just then a beautiful blonde sashays into the bar and the guy says to the bartender, 'You know, I could sure go for a bit of pussy right now.' The bartender smiles again, goes to the fruit bowl, and brings back yet another apple. The guy grins and takes a bite.

'Yuck! Yuck, man. That tastes like shit!' The bartender smiles and says, 'Turn it around.'

A guy goes into a car carrying a briefcase. Being curious, the bartender says, 'Hey mate, what's in the case?'

Without a word, the guy opens the case and a little man, only a foot high, leaps out. He runs to the piano, tunes it, and begins to play. He is a wonderful musician, and pretty soon the bar is full of people and the bartender sells more beer than he has for the entire previous month.

'Hey, your little man is fantastic!' he says to the guy with the case. 'Where did you get him?'

'Well I came across a genie bottle one day in the Amazon forest, and the genie granted me one wish.'

'Wow,' says the bartender. 'I wouldn't mind having a wish or two from a genie. Do you think I could find the bottle?'

'Oh sure,' says the guy, 'but I have to warn you that when you make your wish you'll have to speak very slowly and pronounce everything very clearly.'

'Well, it works, doesn't it? asks the bartender. 'You got your wish didn't you?'

'Tell me,' replies the guy man wearily, 'do you really think I would wish for a twelve-inch pianist?'

★

FUN THINGS TO DO WHILE WAITING FOR A FREE TOILET CUBICLE

1. Start crossing your legs and squirm desperately, while edging your way closer to the person next to you.

2. Go to the hand towel dispenser and yank a whole heap out and distribute them around, charging 20 cents per wad.

3. Get down on your hands and knees and start peering under the cubicle doors, calling out gleefully, 'I can see you!'

4. Shake hands with everyone in line and tell them this is your fourth visit today.

5. Frown, sigh, and mutter, 'Gotta go, gotta go!' Then pause, grimace, and say, 'Oops!'

6. Talk about the new brand of toilet paper you have discovered.

7. Get out your lunch and start eating.

Joel: 'What's the difference between a
shower curtain and toilet paper?'
Adrian: 'I don't know.'
Joel: 'Oh, so it was you!'

★

Three men checked into a hotel. The clerk at the counter told them there was only one room left so the men decided to all share the bed. Next morning, the man that slept on the right side of the bed said, 'I had a really weird dream. I dreamt that someone jerked me off.' 'That's weird,' said the guy on the left side of the bed, 'I also dreamt that someone jerked me off.'

The man in the middle said, 'I had a different dream, I dreamt that I went skiing.'

★

For many months Jim wished that he and Jen would 'get down to business', but he felt a bit shy about broaching the subject. One evening, however, he and Jen were enjoying a romantic dinner down on her parents' farm. The mood seemed right – even the silhouette of a bull humping a cow in the distance seemed to be telling Jim that this was the right moment to finally bring up the subject. He took her hand gently and whispered in her ear, 'I'd sure like to be doing what that bull is doing.'

'Well, why don't you,' she whispered back. 'Dad's been away, so I'm sure the cow would be happy to.'

What did the leper say to the prostitute?
You can keep the tip.

How can you tell which is the head nurse?
She's the one with the dirty knees.

Big Hawk the Indian was with the park ranger one day when they got lost. The park ranger says to Big Hawk, 'Use your tracking ability to get us out of this mess.' Big Hawk bends down and puts his ear to the ground. 'Buffalo come.' The park ranger replies, 'How do you know?' Big Hawk says, 'Ear sticky.'

★

Some crooks break their way into a bank vault and find hundreds of safes. They open the first safe and the only thing they find in there is a vanilla pudding. The head crook says, 'I'm hungry.' So they eat the pudding. They open up the second safe and there's another vanilla pudding. So they devour it too. Safe after safe, no money, only pudding. After all the safes had been opened, they were starting to feel ill from all that pudding. 'Well,' they say, 'we didn't get any money, but at least we won't have to buy dinner tonight!' The next day on the news they hear: 'Yesterday the biggest sperm bank in the world was robbed....'

★

A leper walks into a bar and orders a beer. When the bartender brings it out and sets it down in front of him, the bartender suddenly throws up. The leper says, 'What's up? Does my appearance bother you? I can leave if there's a problem.'

'No, no! No problem. Look, I'll get you another beer.' So the bartender cleans up his mess, pulls another beer, sets it down in front of the leper, and throws up again.

'Are you sure there's no problem with me being here?' the leper asks.

'No, no problem,' the bartender says. 'It won't happen again. I'll go get you another beer.' So he cleans up his mess, gets another beer, and throws up AGAIN.

'Look, you obviously don't want me here in your bar. Why didn't you just say so? I would have left straightaway!' shouts the leper, who at this point is very angry.

'Sir, I am very sorry,' apologises the bartender, 'but it's not you. It's the guy next to you dipping his corn chips in your arm...'

★

Tali and Foley were having dinner at a restaurant one night when Tali noticed a spoon in their waiter's apron. Tali didn't think too much of this until another waiter came over with glasses of water; he, too, sported a spoon in his apron. Tali told Foley of her observation, and as they both looked around the room, they could see that all the waiters had spoons in their aprons. When the first waiter returned to take their order, Tali asked, 'Why the spoons?' 'Well,' explained the waiter, 'this place is under new management, and our new boss has all these fantastic ideas about how to improve efficiency. Apparently he read some study about how patrons drop spoons on the floor 80 percent more often than any other utensil. So now we all carry a spoon with us to cut down our trips to the kitchen and save time.' Just as he concluded, a 'ch-ching' came from the table behind him, and he quickly replaced the fallen spoon with the one from his pocket. 'I'll grab another spoon the next time I'm in the kitchen instead of making a special trip,' he proudly explained. Tali and Foley were both impressed, and sat back to wait for their meal. When the waiter came over again to bring them their steaks, Foley noticed a black plastic cord protruding from the waiter's fly. A quick look around the room revealed that a similar piece of cord dangled out of each waiter's fly.

'Excuse me,' said Foley to their waiter, a little embarrassed. 'What's the deal with the cord hanging out of your fly?'

'Oh, that,' smiled the waiter. 'That's another good idea the new boss came up with to save time in the bathroom.'

'How's that?'

'You see, we use the cord to pull out our dicks at the urinals and thereby eliminate the need to wash our hands, cutting time spent in the bathroom by over 95 percent!'

'Oh, that makes sense,' said Foley, thinking through the process. 'Hey, wait a minute. If the cord helps you pull it out, how do you get it back in?'

'Well,' the waiter whispered, 'I don't know about the other guys, but I use my spoon.'

Did you hear about the cross-eyed circumciser?
He got the sack.

Did you hear about the male prostitute who contracted leprosy?
He did okay for a while, and then his business dropped off.

A ventriloquist walked into an Auckland town and saw a farmer with his dog.

Ventriloquist: 'Hey, cool dog. Mind if I speak to him?'

Farmer: 'Dogs don't talk!'

Ventriloquist: 'Hey dog, how's it going?'

Dog: 'Not bad, not bad.'

Farmer: (Look of disbelief)

Ventriloquist: 'Is this your owner?' (pointing at the farmer)

Dog: 'Yep.'

Ventriloquist: 'Does he treat you well?'

Dog: 'Yeah, great. He walks me every day, feeds me great food, couldn't be better.'

Farmer: (Look of disbelief)

Ventriloquist: 'Mind if I talk to your horse?'

Farmer: 'Horses don't talk!'

Ventriloquist: 'Hey horse, how's it going?'

Horse: 'Not bad, not bad.'

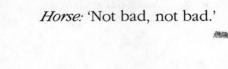

Farmer: (Look of disbelief)

Ventriloquist: 'Is this your owner?'
(Pointing at the farmer)

Horse: 'Yep.'

Ventriloquist: 'How's he treat you?'

Horse: 'Really well. Lots of fresh hay and oats, he rides me every day, and the water is always clean.'

Farmer: (Look of disbelief)

Ventriloquist: 'Mind if I talk to your SHEEP?'

Farmer: (Stuttering, and hardly able to talk)....
'Th-Th-Them sheep ain't nothing but liars!'

★

A tourist dining in a five star restaurant noticed that the waiter had his thumb in every dish he served. When the chicken soup came out, the waiter's thumb was resting in it, when the lamb casserole was brought to the table, the waiter's thumb was in it, and when the hot apple pie for dessert was brought out, again, the waiter's thumb was in it.

'What's going on here?' demanded the tourist. 'You've had your thumb in every dish I've been brought. It's disgusting.' The waiter said, 'I have arthritis in my thumb and must keep it warm.'

The tourist was furious. 'You filthy bastard, putting your thumb in my food. Why don't you stick it up your arse!'

'I do,' replied the waiter. 'In the kitchen.'

A guy comes home to his wife with a big bunch of flowers and she says, 'I suppose this means I have to keep my legs open for the next three days!'

The husband replies, 'Why? Don't you have any vases?'

What did one lesbian frog say to the other?
Gee, we really do taste like chicken.

★

A guy walks into a club and sits down.
He starts dialling numbers on his hand, as if
using a telephone, then holds an animated
discussion with his fingers. The club owner
notices and walks up to him. 'Listen, buddy.
This is a rough club. I don't want any fights
breaking out here, so you better stop that
funny business of yours.'
The guy says, 'Look, mate. I'm not trying to
start anything. I'm just a hi-tech bloke. I've had
a phone inserted into my hand so I can always
be contacted. Whenever my wife or agent want
to call me, they can, without the batteries
dying. By the way, where's the bathroom?' The

club owner points the way and the guy walks off. After 20 minutes go by and the guy hasn't emerged from the bathroom the club owner starts to get a little worried. After all, the club attracted some rather nasty people sometimes. Fearing the worst, he goes into the bathroom. He finds the guy leaning towards the wall, spread-eagled. His pants are pulled down and he has a roll of toilet paper sticking out of his butt.

'Oh shit!' said the club owner. 'Did they rob you? Are you hurt?'

The guy turns and says, 'Oh, I'm fine. I'm just waiting for a fax.'

★

Two unemployed men are bumming
around town when Man #1 says, 'I'd
really like a night on the booze, but I don't
think $2 is gonna stretch that far.'
Man #2 replies, 'Alright. I've got a plan.
We start with buying a hotdog.'
Man #1 asks quizzically, 'And how
is that going to help?'
Man #2 replies, 'Well, we get the
hotdog and throw away the roll. Then I'll
take the sausage and put it down my pants
and we go to a bar. We order some drinks,
and when the bartender asks for his money,
I'll pull down my zipper. You drop to
your knee and act like you're having a
real good time down there, and the
barkeeper will throw us out for being
faggots, and we won't have to pay.'
Man #1 agrees. So they go into a bar, order
some drinks, and gulp them down.
When the bartender says, 'That'll be $8.50,'
Man #2 drops his pants and pulls out the
sausage. Man #1 drops to his knees and
starts sucking on it. The bartender
immediately throws them out of his pub.
The two then visit several more bars, pulling
off the same trick. After the seventh bar Man

#1 finally says, 'Mate, we've gotta stop this. My knees are killing me!'

Man #2 replies, 'You think that's bad, I lost the sausage after the third bar.'

★

A male and female whale were out for a romantic swim one sunny day when they saw a whaling ship. The male whale said to the female: 'Let's go and blow out our air holes at the same time so the ship will sink.' So they went over and did it. Sure enough, the ship capsized and sank. But the sailors found their way out and were swimming to shore. Furious, the male whale said to the female, 'Let's chase them and eat them before they get to shore!' But this time his companion was not so keen. 'Look,' she said. 'I went along with the blowjob, but I absolutely refuse to swallow the seamen.'

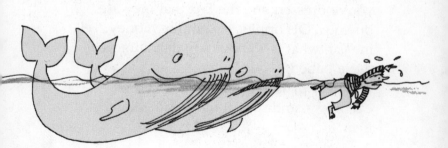

★

What did the cannibal do after he dumped his girlfriend?
Wiped his arse.

One night a bartender notices this hideous guy at the far end of the bar with several hot women around him. The bartender says to him, 'Please don't get offended when I tell you this, but I couldn't help noticing you have several beautiful women hanging all over you, and, forgive me, but you are not exactly the most handsome person I've ever seen. In fact, you're quite ugly. Now, normally, I would think these ladies are attracted to you because of your money, but I can tell by the way you're dressed and the fact that they are buying YOU drinks, it's not the money. Tell me, sir, what is it about you that attracts all these babes?'

The man paused a moment, licked his eyebrows, and said, 'I haven't the faintest idea.'

How do you embarrass an archeologist?
*Give him a used tampon and ask him which
period it came from.*

★

A man wakes up early the day of his birthday and nudges his wife. 'So what did you get me?' The wife, horrified because she had completely forgotten it was his birthday, said, 'Today, because it's your birthday, I'll grant you one favour. So ask away.'

Being a reasonable man, he says to his wife, 'Alrighty love. You've got three choices. One, you can go to the races with me. Two, you can let me stick it up your arse, or three, you can give me a blowjob. Now I'm gonna get ready and stick the dog in the truck. Make up your mind before I get back.'

Hubby returns twenty minutes later and says, 'Well, what's it gonna be?'

She says, 'Well, you know I hate going to the races so I'm not doing that. There's no way I'm letting you up my arse so I guess it's a blowjob for you, birthday boy.'

A few seconds later as she gets down to the deed she immediately begins choking and spluttering. 'Christ, you taste like shit!'

'Oh yeah,' the husband replies, 'The dog didn't want to come to the races either.'

The Hospital Director was showing a nun around his hospital in the hope of receiving a donation from the church. 'And this is B wing,' said the director, as they passed a room where they could see a man masturbating wildly. Naturally the nun was very shocked by this and demanded an explanation as to why these activities were allowed in the hospital. 'Ah,' said the director. 'That poor patient is suffering from quite a horrible disease. He produces so much sperm that unless he gets rid of it five times a day his testicles will explode.'

'Oh,' said the nun. 'Well I guess I can understand.' They continued through B wing and opened the door to C wing. The nun peeked into the first room they passed and saw a nurse, on her knees, giving a patient a blow job. 'Oh, my God!' she shrieked. 'I demand an explanation for this!'

The doctor said. 'Same problem, better health insurance.'

★

There was once a young couple, Sarah and Alex, who married and looked like they were going to be one of those happily ever after types until it occurs to Sarah that they hardly ever had sex anymore. In fact, she can't even remember the last time they did the deed, and it troubles her. She suspects the problem lay with Alex's trips to the pub – every night after work he would come home, get changed, go out with his mates, get completely sozzled, and return home too drunk to do anything. One particular night Sarah decides it's about time she made a real effort to fix the situation. So she sits down provocatively on the couch in her skimpiest, sexiest dress, and waits for him to get home.

As always, when Alex arrives he gets changed and goes to the pub, with barely a glance at Sarah. Rejected again, she remains where she is on the couch and stares at the floor. But two hours later (long before he normally gets home) she hears Alex coming in. Sarah quickly assumes a sexy pose, and to her relief and surprise Alex's first words are, 'Go on, get into the bedroom.'

'Yay,' she thinks, 'about bloody time I get a bit of a romp!'

When Sarah gets to the bedroom, she removes all her clothing and sits on the edge of the bed. Alex comes in and says, 'Alright, get in front of the mirror...'

Kinky...she's really excited now.
'...and do a handstand.'
'Oh God, this is gonna be good!' she thinks.
Alex walks over to Sarah, parts her legs and
places his chin in her crotch and...
'Damn, the blokes are right. A beard *wouldn't*
suit me...!'

★

Sammy was hired to play guitar for a movie score. He couldn't wait to see the finished film and hear his music. He asked the producer where he could catch the film. The producer explained that the music was for a porno flick, and told Sammy where it was showing. So, in disguise Sammy went to see the film. Hoping no one would recognise him he slunk to the back of the cinema, and sat next to an elderly couple who also appeared to be in disguise. The movie started, and it was the filthiest, most perverse porno flick ever. The lead character was an attractive woman who was into group sex, S & M, the works. Very embarrassed and blushing, Sammy turned to the old couple and whispered, 'I'm really not into the sick stuff. I'm just here for the music.'

The woman turned to Sammy and whispered back, 'That's okay, we're just here to see our daughter.'

A woman dies and goes to heaven. While in line, she hears a bloodcurdling scream, very unheaven-like indeed. Very disturbed, she floats over to St Peter to see what the deal is. 'Oh, that's just that woman over there. They're drilling holes in her back so they can attach wings to her.' The woman is taken aback by this, and while thinking about it the screaming starts again. It's even louder and more horrific than before. The woman looks questioningly at St Peter.

'Oh, now they're just drilling holes in the back of her head to attach her halo.' At this, the woman tells St Peter she'd rather go to hell.

'Are you sure?' he asks. 'It's terrible there! You'll be sodomised and raped!'

'That's okay,' says the woman, 'I already have the holes for that!'

Now there's this guy who owns a stud farm, and one day a midget calls in, hoping to buy a horse. He walks up, and the owner asks him if he wants a male or female horse.

'A female horth,' the midget says. *That's quite a speech impediment*, the farm owner thinks. So anyway, the owner shows him one of his best fillies.

'Nithe horth, can I thee into her mouth?' the midget asks. So the owner picks up the midget and shows him the horse's mouth.

'Nithe mouth. Can I thee her eyeth?'

So the owner picks up the midget and shows him her eyes.

'What about the earth?' Now the owner is a bit fed up, but he picks up the midget one more

time and shows him the horse's ears.
'Okay, finally, I'd like to thee her twat.' With
that, the owner picks up the midget and
shoves his head up the horse's twat, then
pulls him out.
Feeling totally disgusted and sick, the midget
says, 'Perhapth I thould thay it diffwently. I'd
like to thee her run!'

One cold and bleak morning a man is driving
through the country. Suddenly from out of
nowhere, a massive bald man steps on the
road. He's seven foot tall, and his muscles
ripple in every inch of his body. At the
roadside there also stands a young woman.
She is absolutely beautiful – slim, shapely, fair
complexion, golden hair ... heart stopping. The
driver stops and stares, and his attention is only
distracted from the lovely girl when the
monster opens the car door and drags him
from his seat with a fist resembling a raw ham.
'Right,' he shouts, 'Ah want you to masturbate.'
'But...' stammers the driver.
'Do it now...or I'll bloody kill yer!'
So the driver turns his back on the girl, drops
his trousers and starts to masturbate. Thinking
of the girl on the roadside this doesn't take him
long. 'Right,' snarls Mr Tough. 'Do it again!'

'But...' protests the driver.

'Now!'

So the driver does it again.

'Right mate, do it again,' demands Mr Tough.
This goes on for nearly two hours. The
hapless driver gets cramps in both arms, he has
rubbed himself raw, has violent knob-ache,
and despite the cold wind has collapsed in a
sweating, jibbering heap on the ground,
unable to stand. 'Do it again,' says Mr Tough.

'I can't do it anymore – you'll just have to kill
me,' whimpers the man.

Mr Tough looks down at the pathetic soul
slumped on the roadside.

'Okay, mate,' he says. '*Now* you can give my
daughter a lift to the next town.'

★

A little girl runs out to the garage where her father is working on his car, and asks him, 'Daddy, what's sex?' So her father sits her down, and tells her all about the birds and the bees. He tells her about conception, sexual intercourse, sperm and eggs. He tells her about puberty, menstruation, erections, wet dreams. He thinks, what the hell, and goes on to tell her the works. He describes masturbation, anal and oral sex, group sex, bondage and discipline, homosexuality, sex toys ... you name it. The girl is somewhat awe-struck with this sudden influx of bizarre new knowledge, and her father finally asks, 'So why did you want to know about sex?' 'Oh, Mummy said lunch would be ready in a couple of secs...'

Confucius say...
He who walk through airport door sideways, going to Bangkok.

Confucius say...
Boy who sleep with stiff problem wake up with solution in hand.

★

Confucius say...
Girl who sits on Judge's lap gets honorable discharge.

Confucius say...
Lady who go camping must beware of evil intent.

Confucius say...
Man who keep feet firmly on ground have trouble putting on pants.

Confucius say...
Man who stand on street corner with hands in pockets, not feeling crazy, feeling nuts.

Confucius say...
Man with tight trousers is pressing his luck.

Confucius say...
He who fishes in others' holes often catches crabs.

Confucius say...
Man who go to sleep with itchy bum wake up with smelly finger.

One day, Pinocchio and his girlfriend were in bed doing what girls and wooden boys do. As they were cuddling later, Pinocchio could tell that something was bothering his girlfriend. So, he asked her, 'What's the matter, honey?' Pinocchio's girlfriend gave a big sigh and replied, 'You're probably the best guy I've ever met, but every time we make love you give me splinters.' This remark bothered Pinocchio a great deal, so the next day he went to seek advice from his creator, Gepetto. After listening to the problem, Gepetto handed over a square of sandpaper and said, 'Now this should smooth out the problem!' Gratefully, Pinocchio took the sandpaper and went off to try it. Now, a few weeks passed by and Gepetto was in town to have some blades sharpened at the hardware store when he ran into Pinocchio.

Pinocchio was buying up ALL of the sandpaper in the hardware store, so Gepetto remarked, 'So, Pinocchio, things must be going pretty damn well with you and the girls.'
Pinocchio replied, 'Girls? Who needs girls?'

A guy, his dog, and a pig are the only survivors of a terrible shipwreck, and they find themselves stranded on a desert island. A few slow weeks pass by. Every evening they'd lie out on the beach and watch the stars. One night the guy was feeling a little amorous and the pig started to look like not such a bad prospect after all. So the guy rolled toward the pig and put his around it. The dog was quite jealous about this and growled until the guy took his arm away. A few weeks passed by, and lo and behold, there was another shipwreck. The only survivor was a beautiful young woman, with a perfect hourglass figure. Luckily she was uninjured. She got along well with the others and went to the beach with them every evening. One night the guy began getting 'those' ideas again, so he leaned across to the girl and said, 'Umm, would you mind taking the dog for a walk?'

★

It being the nineties and all, the man decided he would have a facelift for his birthday. It costs him $5,000, and he is ecstatic about the result. He looks fantastic! On the way home he stops at a milk bar to buy some lollies and says to the girl serving him, 'How old do you think I am?'

'Hmm, about 33,' was the reply.

'I'm actually 45!' the man says, feeling really happy. After that he goes into McDonalds for lunch, and asks the sales assistant there the same question. Her reply is even better...'Oh, you look about 30.' The man is now feeling very pleased with himself indeed. While standing at the bus stop he asks an old bag lady the same question. She croaks, 'I am 90 years old, and my eyesight is not what it once was, but when I was young there was a sure way of telling how old a man is. If I put my hand down your pants and play with your balls for ten minutes I will be able to tell your exact age.' As there was no one around, the man thought what the hell and let her slip her wrinkled hand down his pants and have a good rummage around. Ten minutes later the old lady says, 'Okay, it's done. You are 45.' Stunned, the man says, 'That was brilliant! How did you do that?' The old lady replies, 'I was behind you in McDonalds.'

★

A doctor had the reputation of helping couples increase the joy in their sex life, but always promised not to take a case if he felt he could not help them. Mr and Mrs Adams went to see the doctor, and he gave them thorough physical exams, psychological exams, and various tests and then concluded, 'Yes, I am happy to say that I believe I can help you. On your way home from my office stop at the supermarket and buy some grapes and some donuts. Go home, take off your clothes, and you, sir, roll the grapes across the floor until you make a bulls eye in your wife's love canal. Then on hands and knees you must crawl to her like a leopard and retrieve the grape using only your tongue. Then next, ma'am, you must take the donuts and from across the room, toss them at your husband until you make a ringer around his love pole. Then like a lioness, you must crawl to him and eat a donut.'

The couple went home and their sex life improved out of sight. They told their friends, Mr and Mrs Rainard, that they should see the good doctor. The doctor greeted the Rainards and warned he would not take the case unless he felt that he could help them; so he conducted the physical exams and the same battery of tests.

Then he told the Rainards the bad news. 'I can't help you, so I will not take your money. I believe your sex life is as good as it will ever be. I'm sorry.'

The Rainards pleaded with him, and said, 'You helped our friends, now please, please help us.'

'Well, okay,' the doctor said. 'On your way home from the office, stop at the supermarket and buy some apples and a box of Froot Loops...'

An old man and an old lady are getting ready for bed one night when all of a sudden the woman bursts out of the bathroom, flings open her robe and yells: 'Super Pussy!'

The old man says: 'I'll have the soup.'

Modern Technology

Who is General Failure and why is he reading my hard disk?

★

Bill Gates dies and is ready to enter the afterlife. He meets St Peter at the Pearly Gates, who looks a little confused. 'I don't know if I should let you in here, Bill. I mean, sure, you helped bring computers to the world, but then, you also created that Windows 95 crap. I can't decide where I should put you. I know this is against procedure and all, but I think maybe I'll let YOU choose. I'll let you check out both places for a couple of minutes so you can make up your mind.'

'Okay then,' said Bill, 'I'll try Hell first.' So off Bill went to Hell. Hell was beautiful. The weather was warm, the sun was shining, and there were lots of bikini-clad women frolicking about. He was ecstatic. 'This is great!' he told St Peter. 'I love it here! But I guess I should have a look at Heaven, though I doubt it could be any better.' The two flew up in the sky to Heaven, where angels drifted about, singing beautiful songs and smiling at everyone. It was a very peaceful and serene place. Still, it wasn't

as enticing as Hell, and Bill didn't need to
think long. 'I think I'd prefer Hell,' he said.
'Fine,' replied St Peter. So Bill Gates went to
Hell. Two weeks later, St Peter decided to
check on the late billionaire to see how he was
doing. When he entered the gates of Hell he
found Bill shackled to a wall, screaming in
pain as hot flames licked his body and demons
prodded him with sharp knives.
'How's everything going?' St Peter asked. Bill
gasped in anguish, 'This is awful! This is
nothing like the Hell I visited two weeks ago!
I can't believe this is happening! What
happened to that other place, with the
beautiful beaches and the scantily clad women
playing in the water?'
'That was a demo version,' replied St Peter.

How many Tech Support people does it take to
change a light bulb?
*Have you looked at the user manual? I'm not
going to help you until you've looked at the
user manual. Bloody light bulb users ...
shouldn't be allowed to have one if they don't
know how to use them!*

COMPUTER VIRUSES

Bulimia Virus – eats up all your files then spews them out all mixed up.

Pro-Life Virus – won't let you delete a file no matter how unwanted it is.

Pro-Choice Virus – gives you a choice about whether or not to delete a file, even when it knows you definitely want to delete it.

Gynaecologist Virus – invades your system where you don't want it to.

Elvis Virus – your computer gets slow and lazy, and makes horrible sounds.

Alien Virus – invades your system in places where no virus has ever been before.

Consultant Virus – tests your system then sends you a bill for $750.

★

How many programmers does it take to change a light bulb?
That's impossible, it's a hardware problem.

How many database programmers does it take to change a light bulb?
Three. One to write the dead light bulb removal script, one to write the new light bulb insertion script, and one to act as a light bulb administrator to make sure nobody else tries to change the light bulb at the same time.

TOP 10 REASONS COMPUTERS MUST BE FEMALE

1. They sometimes just sit there, blinking dumbly at you.

2. No one but their creator understands their internal logic.

3. Even your smallest mistakes are immediately committed to memory for future reference.

4. The message, 'There is a General Application Error,' is about as informative as, 'If you don't know why I'm mad at you, then I'm certainly not going to tell you.'

5. They frustrate the hell out of you when you give a command and they don't, won't, or can't follow it.

6. Sometimes, try as you might, you can't turn them on, particularly if you already have a floppy in.

7. If your floppy disk has a virus, you can be damn sure your computer will get it.

8. They sometimes suffer communication problems. They won't talk to the printer, won't acknowledge the modem's presence, and won't write to the hard disk.

9. You continually have to talk to the supplier, which you really don't want to do.

10. If you write a programme wrong it can start an endless loop and just go on and on and on and on...

★

TOP 10 REASONS COMPUTERS
MUST BE MALE

1. They have a lot of data, but are still clueless.

2. A better model is always just around the corner.

3. They look nice and shiny until you bring them home.

4. It is always necessary to have a backup.

5. They'll do whatever you say if you push the right buttons.

6. The best part of having either one is the games you can play.

7. In order to get their attention, you have to turn them on.

8. The lights are on, but nobody's home.

9. Big power surges knock them out for the night.

10. Size does matter.

★

REASONS WHY E-MAIL IS LIKE A PENIS

1. Those who have it would be devastated if it were ever cut off.

2. Many of those who don't have it would like to try having it (e-mail envy).

3. If you're not careful, it can spread viruses.

4. If you use it too much, you'll find it becomes more and more difficult to think coherently.

5. Everyone thinks it's far more important than it actually is.

6. If you're not careful, it has a way of getting you into lots of trouble.

7. When the system is down, no one is happy.

8. If an email comes with a virus, it can wreak havoc with the whole system and make you wary of using it again.

★

It is the year 2087. The United Nations have finally finished designing a super intelligent computer that can deal with any problem. Military leaders are huddled around the new machine. They describe the latest happenings and the strategic plans they have engineered in order to beat the enemy. They ask the computer, 'Shall we attack now? Or retreat?' The computer computes for the next day and a half and comes up with the answer, 'Yes!' 'Yes, what?' asks one of the generals, stupefied. After another half a day, the computer replies, 'Yes, sir!'

★

A tourist is looking around a pet shop, when a bloke walks in and says to the shopkeeper, 'I'll have a C monkey, thanks.' The shopkeeper takes a monkey out of a cage and says, 'That's $2000 mate.' The customer hands over the money and walks out with the monkey.
Curious, the tourist says to the shopkeeper, 'I had no idea monkeys were so expensive!'
The shopkeeper replies, 'Well, that monkey can progam in C, so he's well worth the money.' The tourist points to another monkey. 'What about that one, then? He's $5000 – what does he do?'
'Oh, he's a C++ monkey. He can do some amazingly useful stuff.'
The tourist nods, and then notices yet another monkey – this one with a $50,000 price tag. He gasps, 'Oh my god, that one costs a fortune! What does he do?'
'Well, I haven't actually seen him do anything yet,' replies the shopkeeper, 'but he says he's a contractor.'

Just imagine what would happen if people behaved the same way with their cars as they do with computers?

HELPLINE: Motoring Helpline, how can I help you?

CUSTOMER: I got in my car and closed the door, and nothing happened!

HELPLINE: Did you put the key in the ignition and turn it?

CUSTOMER: What's an ignition?

HELPLINE: It's a starter motor that draws current from your battery and turns over the engine.

CUSTOMER: Ignition? Motor? Battery? Engine? How come I have to know all of these technical terms just to use my car?

HELPLINE: Motoring Helpline, how can I help you?

CUSTOMER: My car ran fine for a week, and now it won't go anywhere!

HELPLINE: Is the petrol tank empty?

CUSTOMER: Huh? How do I know!?

HELPLINE: There's a little gauge on the front panel, with a needle, and markings from 'E' to 'F.' Where is the needle pointing?

CUSTOMER: It's pointing to 'E.' What does that mean?

HELPLINE: It means that you have to go to the petrol station, and buy some more petrol. You can install it yourself, or pay the man to install it for you.

CUSTOMER: What!? I paid $20,000 for this car! Now you tell me that I have to keep buying more components? I want a car that comes with everything built in!

HELPLINE: Motoring Helpline, how can I help you?

CUSTOMER: Your cars suck!

HELPLINE: What's wrong?

CUSTOMER: It crashed, that's what went wrong!

HELPLINE: What were you doing?

CUSTOMER: I wanted to run faster, so I pushed the accelerator pedal all the way to the floor. It worked for a while, and then it crashed — and now it won't start!

HELPLINE: It's your responsibility if you misuse the product. What do you expect us to do about it?

CUSTOMER: I want you to send me one of the latest versions that doesn't crash anymore!

HELPLINE: Motoring Helpline, how can I help you?

CUSTOMER: Hi! I just bought my first car, and I chose your car because it has automatic transmission, cruise control, power steering, power brakes, and power door locks.

HELPLINE: Thanks for buying our car. How can I help you?

CUSTOMER: How do I work it?

HELPLINE: Do you know how to drive?

CUSTOMER: Do I know how to what?

HELPLINE: Do you know how to DRIVE?

CUSTOMER: I'm not a technical person! I just want to go places in my car!

★

YOU KNOW YOU ARE AN
EMAIL JUNKIE IF ....

1. You get a tattoo that reads 'This hip best viewed with Netscape Navigator 1.1 or higher.'

2. You turn off your modem and get this awful empty feeling, like you just pulled the plug on a loved one.

3. You decide to stay at uni for an additional year or two, just for the free Internet access.

4. You laugh at people with 9600-baud modems.

5. You start using smileys in your snail mail.

6. You suffer anxiety when you don't have access to your computer. You start to twitch. You pick up the phone and manually dial your ISP's access number. You try to hum to communicate with the modem.... And you succeed.

7. You start introducing yourself as 'Mal dot net dot au.'

8. All of your friends have an @ in their names.

9. Your cat has its own home page.

10. You can't call your mother... she doesn't have a modem.

11. You check your mail. It says 'no new messages.' So you check it again.

12. You start tilting your head sideways to smile.

13. You don't know what sex three of your closest friends are, because they have neutral user names and you never bothered to find out.

14. You move into a new house and decide to Netscape before you landscape.

15. You tell the taxi driver you live at 'http://www.365.big.house/rendered.html.'

15 THINGS YOU LEARN ABOUT COMPUTERS FROM THE MOVIES

1. You never have to use the spacebar when typing long sentences.

2. All monitors are readable from six feet away.

3. You can gain access to any information you want by simply typing ACCESS ALL SECRET FILES on any keyboard.

4. Likewise, you can infect a computer with a destructive virus by simply typing UPLOAD VIRUS.

5. Computer operators never make typos at crucial moments.

6. All computers, in every lab and office, are connected. You can access the information on the villain's desktop computer, even if it's turned off.

7. Powerful computers beep whenever you press a key or the screen changes. Some computers also slow down the output on the screen so that it doesn't go faster than you can read.

8. People typing away on a computer will turn it off without saving the data.

9. A hacker can get into the most sensitive computer in the world before intermission and guess the secret password in two tries.

10. Any PERMISSION DENIED has an OVERRIDE function.

11. Complex calculations and loading of huge amounts of data will be accomplished in under three seconds.

12. When the power plant/missile site/computer lab overheats, all the control panels will explode, as will the entire building.

13. No matter what kind of computer disk it is, it'll be readable by any system you put it into.

14. Computers never crash during key, high-intensity activities.

15. The more high-tech the equipment, the more buttons it has. However, everyone must have been highly trained, because the buttons aren't labelled.

Last year, I upgraded my GirlFriend 4.0 to GirlFriend 4.1. This software package then later installed itself as Fiancee 1.0. Recently, I upgraded Fiancee 1.0 to Wife 1.0 and it's a real memory hog. It has taken up all my space, and Wife 1.0 must be running before I can do ANYTHING. It is also spawning Child Processes which are further consuming system resources. Some applications, such as PokerNight 9.0, BeerBash 6.5, and PubNight 7.0 are no longer able to run in the system at all. Additional plug-ins were automatically installed without me acquiescing, such as Mother-In-Law 1.0, and there is no uninstall feature for these plug-ins. No mention of these behaviours was discussed in the brochures or documentation, although other users have reported similar problems. Because of this, some users that I know have decided to avoid the headaches associated with these upgrades, and simply move from Girlfriend 4.0 to Girlfriend 5.0. Unfortunately, this is not without peril as well, as all traces of Girlfriend 4.0 must be removed from the system before attempting installation of 5.0. Even then, Girlfriend 5.0 will repeatedly run system checks (usually in the background, and often late at night when the system is asleep) to find evidence of previous versions. To cap it off, Girlfriend 5.0 has a nag feature reminding about the advantages of upgrading to Wife 1.0.

However, I do like some of the features that you are planning to include in the upcoming Girlfriend 5.1 release:

A 'Don't remind me again' button

A Minimise button

A Shutdown feature

An install shield feature so that Girlfriend can be completely uninstalled if necessary (so you don't lose cache and other objects).

Unfortunately, since I've already upgraded to Wife 1.0, I don't think I will be able to take advantage of any of these new features, unless you decide to include them in the next Mistress release. But, of course, there is a whole raft of problems associated with the use of Mistress 1.0 and Wife 1.0 on the same system — most notable are system conflicts and continual disk thrashing, which starts shortly after Wife 1.0 detects Mistress 1.0. Interestingly enough, all versions of PersonalLawyer still work fine. Finally, Wife 1.0 apparently deletes all MSMoney files before uninstalling itself; following that, Mistress 1.1 will refuse to install, claiming insufficient resources. I personally find all these new tools and conflicts to be too confusing and time consuming. I'm sticking with Dog 1.0. It slobbers and chews up the paper, but all in all these bugs are tolerable. It is simple to operate and we get along fine.

Rip-snorting Goodies

The weekly sales meeting of the
encyclopaedia company is in progress and the
sales director is annoyed because they aren't
selling well. 'Wilbur, how many encyclopaedias
have you sold this week?'
'Uhh, three, boss.'
'WHAT! THREE! YOU'RE FIRED, NOW! GET
OUT OF MY SIGHT! What about you Clay?'
'Umm, four, boss.'
'WHAT! FOUR! YOU'RE FIRED, NOW! GET
OUT OF MY SIGHT!'
He then spotted Tim, a new employee.
The director, expecting the worst, said,
'Okay, since it's only your first week, what
have you been able to sell?'
'Th-th-th-three th-th-th-thousand, s-s-s-sir.'
The director was flabbergasted. 'How on earth
did you achieve such an incredible figure?'
'S-s-s-sir, I usually j-j-j-just walk up to
th-th-th-the house and when th-th-th-the owner
asks me wh-wh-wh-what I want, I t-t-t-tell
them: 'Hi-h-h-hi, my name is T-T-Tim and I
s-s-s-sell en-en-en encyclopaedias, now
d-d-d-do you w-w-w-wish to b-b-b-buy one
or shall I j-j-just r-r-r-read it to you?'

★

THE 10 TELLTALE SIGNS OF
ADVANCED PARENTHOOD

1. You find yourself singing nursery rhymes to your kid on the train without feeling silly.

2. You become addicted to Bananas in Pyjamas.

3. You buy toys for your child and play with them before he does.

4. You buy matching clothes for you and your three year old.

5. You find yourself watching G-rated films – and loving them.

6. You want to point a gun to the kid that bullied your son at creche and made him cry.

7. You warn everyone that they can't give your kids any presents that make noise.

8. You hope fish fingers are healthy because it's the only thing your child will eat.

9. You manage not to laugh when your five year old daughter asks for a willy like her brother.

10. You fast-forward through the scene where the Lion King's father dies.

★

THE WORLD'S 10 SHORTEST BOOKS

1. All in a Day's Work – Diary of a Council Worker

2. Exciting Confessions of a Bank Teller

3. Great English Lovers

4. American Book of Shy and Polite People

5. A Journey Through the Mind of a Blonde

6. Logic and Reason – Why Vegetarians Eat Fish and Chicken

7. Career Opportunities for History Majors

8. The Joys of Celibacy

9. Everything Men Know About Women

10. Everything Women Know About Men

A photographer from an environmental magazine was assigned to cover a fire that had broken out in a large national park. The magazine wanted to show the havoc the fire was creating and the damage it was doing to the trees.

By the time the photographer had taken an interstate plane and hired a car to take him close to the area, it was quite late and he knew he'd better move fast or he wouldn't be able to shoot anything. He hurried to the small strip runway where a small plane had been arranged to take him over the burning area.

He got to the airport, saw a plane warming up, and grabbing his bag, he rushed on to it, shouting, 'Okay, let's go.'

The pilot swung the little plane into the wind, and within minutes they were in the air.

The photographer said, 'Fly over the park and make two or three low passes so I can take some pictures.'

'Why?' asked the pilot.

'Because I am a photographer,' he responded, 'and photographers take photographs.'

The pilot was silent for a moment; finally he stammered, 'You mean you're not the flight instructor?'

The boss was annoyed because, for the third day running, his secretary was late. Finally, when she arrived, an hour late, he said, fuming, 'You should have been here at nine!'

'Why?' she asked. 'What happened?'

Why do mice have such small balls?
*Because so very few of them know
how to dance.*

★

What do council workers and sperm have in
common?
Only one in two million does any work.

★

The new employee needed a cup of coffee.
So he dialled the number of the tea lady but
got the wrong one. When someone picked up
the phone he said, 'Get me a coffee, will ya?'
'Do you know whom you are talking to?' the
other side asked. 'No,' he replied. 'You are
talking to the director of this company,' the
other side replied. The employee asked, 'Do
you know who is talking on this side?'
'No,' the other side replied.
'Good.' And he put the phone down.

★

A regular customer walks in to Tony's Barber
Shop for a haircut. As he snips away, Tony
asks, 'So, any gossip?' The man tells him he's
off for a long-awaited trip to London.
'London?!' Tony says, 'Why would you want to
go there? It's full of Poms and is freezing!
Jesus! Well, how are you getting there?'

'We're flying with FGA,' the man replies.

'FGA?!' yells Tony. 'They're awful. Their planes are old, their flight attendants are ugly and they never run on schedule! So where you staying?'

'We'll be at the downtown QE International.'

'That DUMP?!' says Tony. 'That's the worst hotel in all of England! No heating in the rooms, grotty carpets, way overpriced! What are you gonna do in London?'

The man says, 'We're going to visit the Queen.'

'HA! That's rich!' laughs Tony. 'You and a million others! Bet you don't even catch a glimpse of her.' A month later, the man comes in for a visit. Tony asks, 'Well, how did that trip to London turn out? Betcha FGA gave you the worst flight of your life!'

'No,' answered the man. 'The flight was excellent. Had a gorgeous air hostess and the food was better than anything I have ever eaten.'

'Hmmm,' Tony says, 'Well, I bet the hotel was just like I described.'

'No, quite the opposite! They'd just finished refurbishing. It's the finest hotel in London, now. They gave us the Royal suite for no extra charge!'

'Well,' Tony mumbles, 'I KNOW you didn't get to see the Queen!'

'Actually, we were quite lucky. As we toured Buckingham Palace, a guard tapped me on the shoulder and explained that the Queen likes to personally meet some of her visitors, and if I'd be so kind as to wait, the Queen would come out and say hello. Sure enough, after five minutes the Queen walked through the door and shook my hand. I knelt down as she spoke a few words to me.'

Impressed, Tony asks, 'Tell me, please! What did she say?'

'Oh, not much really. Just, 'Where'd you get that TERRIBLE haircut?'

★

THE 10 THINGS THAT WE WANTED TO HAPPEN IN THE BRADY BUNCH

1. Marsha gets syphilis.

2. Greg gets incurable acne.

3. Jan gets pregnant.

4. Cindy's hair falls out from over bleaching.

5. Sam is caught in bed with Bobby.

6. Cindy loses her lisp.

7. Alice is convicted of child molestation.

8. Peter stops looking like a girl.

9. Tiger is put down for mauling a baby to death.

10. Carol and Mike partner-swap with the next-door neighbours.

The new travel agency in town was running a competition to draw in more customers. The prize, for the one hundredth customer to walk in the store, was a return trip for two to Fiji. Julian, the only travel agent not out to lunch one Friday, noticed an old man and an old woman peering wistfully through the travel agency window at a poster of Fiji on the wall. Knowing that if they walked in they would be the winners, Julian beckoned them in. They came in a little reluctantly as they were pen-sioners and had no money for a holiday. 'Yes?' asked the elderly woman. A big grin burst out on Julian's face as he said, 'Congratulations! You've just won a trip to Fiji!' Well you should have seen the look of amazement on their faces! Julian presented them with the airline tickets and they left, over the moon.

A couple of months later Julian saw the little old lady as he was on his way home from work. 'How was Fiji?' he asked her. 'Did you have a good time?'

'Oh, it was lovely. The weather was beautifully warm, the food sumptuous and the beach was just perfect. But tell me, who was that old codger I had to share the room with?'

Two missionaries in Africa were captured by a tribe of very hostile cannibals who put them in a large pot of water, built a huge fire under it, and left them there. As the water boiled and the heat grew more and more intense, one of the missionaries started to laugh hysterically. The other missionary couldn't believe it! He said, 'What's wrong with you? We're being boiled alive! They're gonna eat us! What could possibly be funny at a time like this?'

The other missionary said with a gleeful smile, 'I just pissed in the soup!'

★

Two marble statues, one a sculpture of a muscly, attractive hunk, and the other a sculpture of a beautiful and shapely princess, had been standing in the city square for several years. They were positioned face to face, in a just-about-to-kiss pose, but the nature of their existence meant that they couldn't move to complete the kiss, or indeed, get up to any other mischief. One summer morning God spoke to them. 'You have been such patient statues, I am going to reward you with half an hour of human life, to do whatever you wish.' Brought to life, the statues shook themselves a bit and then said to each other excitedly, 'Shall we?' They then disappeared into some bushes. Curious passers-by heard a lot of rustling, but were too polite to investigate. After a while they emerged from the bushes hot, flustered and happy. God, feeling glad that things had obviously gone very well between the two, decided to grant them another 15 minutes. 'Why not start all over again?' giggled the marble woman. 'Yes,' agreed the marble man. 'Let's do it again. Only this time I'll hold down the f***ing pigeon and you can shit on it!'

A blind man was walking down the street when his guide dog stopped and peed on his leg. Reaching into his pocket, he took out a biscuit and gave it to the dog. A passer-by who had seen everything was impressed with the man's kindness. 'That's a nice thing to do after what your dog just did.'

'Not really,' replied the blind man. 'I just needed to find out where his mouth is so I can kick him in the balls.'

★

There were two people walking down the street. One was an artist. The other one didn't have a job either.

★

A man sitting by himself in a restaurant asked a waitress passing by for a glass of water. 'How dare you say that to me!' screamed the woman angrily. 'You filthy disgusting pig!' The man, terribly embarrassed by all the stares he was receiving, said softly, 'I was only asking for a drink.' The woman, incensed, shrieked at the top of her lungs, 'Another word and I am calling the police!' Slinking down in his seat, the man hid behind the menu, waiting for a less conspicuous time to sneak out of the restaurant. A few moments later the waitress came to his table and whisperered apologetically, 'Sir, I'm terribly sorry about what I did before. I'm training to be a psychologist and I'm conducting a study on public embarrassment.' The man stared at her for a moment and looking around the restaurant, bellowed, 'Wow! You'd do all that for me for just $2? And you'd do it to every other guy in the restaurant for another $10?'

A solo bushwalker was asked in a newspaper interview what the most important thing to take on a hiking trip was. 'Well,' he replied. 'When I passed my wilderness training certificate, I was given a first aid box containing a martini-making kit, a mixer, a stirrer, some gin, vermouth and olives. I didn't quite understand its relevance to bushwalking, so one of the blokes took me aside and said, 'Never, ever go bushwalking alone without it. You might be lost out in the wilderness for days or weeks, perhaps a month. Soon, alone and thirsty, you'll remember your martini kit and begin making yourself a martini. Within ten seconds there will be someone at your side saying, "That's not the way to make a martini..."'

Three cool cowboys are sitting around a campfire, telling tall stories. The first says, 'I must be the meanest, toughest cowboy there is. Why, just the other day, a bull got loose and trampled six men before I wrestled it to the ground, by the horns, and killed it with my bare hands.' The second can't stand to be bested. 'Why that's nothing. I was walking down the trail yesterday and an elephant charged right at me. I grabbed it, bit its trunk and tied it up, all with one hand.' The third cowboy remained silent, slowly stirring the coals with his penis.

★

It's 40 degrees in the desert and a man lies exhausted and dying of thirst. He has stripped all his clothes off except his shorts but is still sweating badly from the heat. From out behind a sand dune a salesman appears, staggering under the weight of a load of clean, new, white shirts. Smiling winningly, the salesman tries to sell the dying man a shirt. 'Jesus,' said the man. 'I'm dying of thirst and boiling to death. The last thing I need is a shirt!' The salesman shrugs, bids him farewell, and disappears behind the sand dune. The parched man crawls along the ground, desperately trying to reach a bar he can see in the distance. As he gets closer he can see that there are all types of cool, refreshing drinks to choose from. Mustering up the last of his strength he goes up to the door. 'Sorry,' said the doorman, barring the way. 'You can't come in without a shirt.'

★

A tourist in Vienna visits a graveyard one morning (as you do) and suddenly he hears music. Wondering where it could be coming from, he follows the sound until he locates the origin: the grave of Beethoven. As he reads the headstone, he realises that the music is in fact the famous Ninth Symphony – being played backward! Puzzled, he persuades a friend to return with him that afternoon. By the time they arrive back at the grave, the music has changed. This time it is the Seventh Symphony, and it is also being played backward. Curious, the two friends later return with a music scholar and by this time the Fifth Symphony is playing, yes, backward. The expert points out that the symphonies are being played in the reverse order in which they were composed – first the Ninth, then the Seventh, then the Fifth. Very, very strange. By the next day the word has spread and dozens of people have gathered around the grave, all listening to the Second Symphony being played – you guessed it – backward. Just then a gravedigger walks by, and someone in the crowd asks him if he has an explanation for the music.

'Well it's pretty obvious isn't it?' the gravedigger says incredulously. 'He's decomposing!'

The bishop of a large cathedral sent word through the streets that he was after a new bellringer. A day or so later, the applicants came filing in, and the bishop took each of them up to the belfry to begin the screening process. After interviewing several of them he became tired and was about to call it a day when an armless man approached him and announced he was there to apply for the bellringer's job. The bishop was incredulous. 'But you have no arms!'

'That hinders me not,' said the man. 'Watch!' He then began striking the bells with his face, producing a most beautiful melody. The bishop listened in astonishment, convinced he had found his man. The bellringer rang the bells again, but this time he slipped on something and plunged headlong out of the window and to his death below. The stunned bishop rushed down to the fallen figure, where a crowd had already gathered. As they parted to let the bishop through, one of them asked, 'Bishop, who was this man?'

'I'm not quite sure,' the bishop sadly replied, 'but his face rang a bell.'

(But wait, there's more...)

Although very sad, the following day the bishop continued the interviews. The first man to approach him said, 'Your excellency, I am the brother of the poor, armless wretch who

fell to his death
from this very belfry
yesterday. I pray
that you pay due
homage to his life
by allowing me to
replace him.' The bishop
agreed to give the man an audition, and as the
armless man's brother stooped to pick up a
mallet to strike the first bell, he groaned,
clutched at his chest and died on the spot. Two
monks, hearing the bishop's cries of grief at
this second tragedy, rushed up the stairs to his
side. 'What has happened?' the first asked
breathlessly. 'Who is this man?'
'I don't know his name,' sighed the distraught
bishop, 'but he's a dead ringer for his brother.'

★

Toby was given a parrot for his birthday. Unfortunately, this parrot was one bad-mouthed bird. Every second word was an expletive. Toby tried very hard to change the parrot's ways – he played soft music, read aloud chapters on etiquette, and he never, ever, swore. But nothing worked. One day, the parrot was so rude to one of Toby's friends that Toby cracked it. He shook the bird, getting madder and madder, and when the bird wouldn't shut up, he finally threw it into the freezer for a bit of peace and quiet. For a few moments the parrot squawked and screamed, but then it became silent. Toby, being the good-natured boy that he was, was worried that he may have hurt the parrot, so he quickly opened the freezer door. The parrot gracefully stepped out onto Toby's arm and said very softly, 'I apologise for my offensive language. I will try very, very hard in the future to watch my behaviour and to wash my mouth out with soap if I even think of swearing again.'
Toby was completed amazed at this change of heart. He was just about to ask him what had made the parrot 'see the light' when the parrot spoke again.
'May I ask what the chicken did?'

The manager of a retirement home was collecting the mail one day when two poor guys show up, looking for work. Feeling sorry for them, the manager asks if they'd like to chop some firewood in return for some money. They enthusiastically agree, and the manager goes to the toolshed and finds a couple of axes for them. Some time later, as the manager is in his office, he looks out the window and notices ones of the guys doing some amazing acrobatics on the back lawn. He's jumping in the air, doing cartwheels and swinging form branch to branch. He watches in awe as he swings from a branch, does a flip mid-air, and lands with another cartwheel.

He calls the other guy over to the window and says, 'That friend of yours is marvellous. I'd like him to perform for the senior citizens here – it might pep them up a bit. Do you think he would accept $100?'

'Well,' responds the guy, 'I dunno, I'll have to go ask him.'

'HEY NORM! For $100 WOULD YOU CHOP OFF ANOTHER TOE?'

★

Toe: a device for finding furniture in the dark.

★

10 WAYS TO GET RID OF TELEMARKETERS

1. If they want to lend you money, tell them you just filed for bankruptcy and you could sure use some cash. Ask, 'Do I have to ever pay it back, or is it like the other money I borrowed before my bankruptcy?'

2. If they start out with 'How are you today?' respond with 'I'm so glad you asked, because no one seems to care these days and I have all these problems... my back is playing up, my boils are infected, my cat just died...'

3. Telemarketer: 'Hi, my name is Beth, how are you?' You: 'Oh, my God! Beth, how have you BEEN?' Hopefully, this will give Beth a few brief moments of terror as she tries to figure out where the hell she could know you from.

4. Say 'No' over and over again. Be sure to vary the sound of each no, and keep an even tempo even while they're trying to speak. This is the most fun if you can keep going until they hang up.

5. Let the person go though their spiel, then at the end of it, say in a thick accent, 'I no speaka English.'

6. When they ask for your credit card details, yell hysterically, 'What are you going to do with them? Oh, my God, it's a conspiracy to have me killed!' etc. It should do the trick.

7. Respond to all questions in a quiet, shy voice. When asked for your credit card number, reply in a very small voice that you just couldn't give out anything as personal over the phone as a credit card number... could you perhaps get together over dinner and do it in person?

8. Answer the phone. As soon as you realise it is a telemarketer, hold the receiver a little away from your mouth, make some crashing noises, shout or scream, 'Help! Help!' then hang up.

9. Tell the telemarketer you are busy and if they will give you their phone number you will call them back. If they say they are not allowed to give out their number, ask them for their home number and tell them you will call them at home (this is usually the most effective method of getting rid of telemarketers). If the person says, 'Well, I don't really want to get a call at home,' say, 'Now you know how I feel,' smiling, of course.

10. Say in a slightly slow, sinister voice, 'I know you. I know where you work, I know where you live, I know *everything* about you. Be scared. Be very scared.' It's not nice, but that telemarketer won't bother you anymore.

★

I didn't fight my way to the top of the food chain to be a vegetarian.

★

SHIT

Amish: Old shit is good for the soil, but this modern shit is worthless.

Atheist: I don't believe this shit.

Bureaucrat: I'm sorry, but we can't do this shit until you fill out the form.

Capitalist: Can I sell you some shit?

Catholic: I'm not doing this shit now because it's the wrong time of the month and I don't want any little shits running around.

Christian: When shit happens, pray.

Communist: It's survival of the shittiest.

Evangelist: Send us all your shit.

Existentialist: What is shit anyway?

Islam: If shit happens, take a hostage.

Jehovah's Witness: Knock Knock, I know you shits are home.

Jew: Why does this shit always happen to us?

Mysticist: This is really weird shit. For $300, we can help you get in touch with your inner shit.

Quality Control Inspector: This shit ain't good enough.

Seventh Day Adventist: No shit on Saturdays.

Statistician: There is an 83.7% chance that shit will happen.

★

A penny saved is ridiculous.

★

Any small object when dropped will hide under another object.

★

Confucius say...
Man who wants pretty nurse, must be patient.

★

There once was a man who had a severe digestive problem. Every time he drank malted milk, which unfortunately happened to be his favourite drink ever, he would squeeze out malt-scented farts for the rest of the day. Now, because of this problem, he normally abstained from drinking malted milk, but because it was his birthday, he thought, hey, what the hell, and indulged in two big shakes at lunchtime, with extra malt in each. As he walked home from work, the tirade of bad smells began, and he hoped like anything they would all be out of his system by the time he reached home, for his wife very much disapproved of smelly things. So he farted and fluffed and mockered all the way home. When he arrived there his wife opened the door and said, 'Put on this blindfold. I have a lovely surprise for you,' and he obliged. She led him though the house and sat him down at the table, and just as she was about to remove the blindfold the phone rang. 'Don't move,' she said, and off she went. When she was gone, he seized the opportunity and let go. It was not only loud, but so smelly he had a hard time breathing, so he felt for his napkin and fanned the air about him. As he was wondering if that was the last one, he felt another well of gas build up inside him. He raised his leg and 'rrriiiipppp!' It sounded like a diesel engine revving, and smelled a helluva lot worse. To keep from gagging, he tried waving his arms, hoping to move the smell away from him. Things had just about returned to normal when he felt another urge coming. He shifted his weight to his other leg and let go. This was a real blue ribbon winner; the dishes on the table shook and a couple of pictures fell down from the wall. For the next ten minutes, while he listened to his wife on the phone, he kept up a mega farting session, following each one with a mad fanning of the arms and grunts of disgust at the smell. When he heard his wife returning from the hallway he folded his hands on top of his napkin and tried to regain some composure. Smiling contentedly, he was the picture of innocence when his wife walked in. Apologising for taking so long, she asked if he had peeked at the dinner. After assuring her he had not, she removed the blindfold and yelled, 'Surprise!!' To his extreme and utter horror, there were ten dinner guests seated around the table for his surprise birthday party.

The owner of a market research company was interviewing people for a position which involved going around to houses and talking to people about their opinion of certain products. He was particularly keen to hire one applicant who had a great deal of experience and was very well spoken. The only problem was a disconcerting mannerism: the man seemed to have a nervous tic. Every few seconds his head would shake wildly from side to side. The sales manager decided to be frank. 'You've got all the qualifications for the job and I'd really like to hire you, but I'm afraid that tic of yours might be a problem.'

'No worries,' said the candidate. 'All I need to make it go away is a couple of cough lollies. Look. I'll take some now.' And he began emptying his pockets on the desk. The prospective employer was startled to see dozens of packages of condoms piling up: edible ones, lubricated ones, multicoloured ones, every variety imaginable. 'Aha,' cried the young man happily, 'here they are.' He brandished two lozenges, swallowed them, and sure enough, the head shaking stopped immediately. 'So much for the tic,' said the sales manager sternly, gesturing at the mountain of rubbers, 'but what about all these condoms? I don't want you screwing around on the job.'

'No fear. I'm a happily married man.'

'So how can you account for the contents of your pockets?'

'It's simple, sir. Did you ever go into a pharmacy, shaking your head like crazy, and ask for a packet of cough drops?'

★

A man takes his dalmation to the vet.

'He's been behaving funny lately, and his nose isn't wet anymore.'

The vet picked the dog up and looked at its nose. 'I'm going to have to put him down,' said the vet.

'Why, just because his nose is dry?' asked the man in disbelief.

'No, because he's too f***ing heavy!'

A pig snuffles into a bar and orders a beer. Barman says, 'Hey, you're a pig.'

'Well, strike me down!' says the pig.

'You know what I mean,' says the barman.

'You can talk – that's pretty unusual for a pig.'

'Yeah, well, freaks of nature do happen sometimes,' replies the pig. 'Now gimme a beer will ya?'

The barman serves him up one and asks if he lives in the area.

'Nah, I just work around here – over on the building site actually.' The barman nods and they chat a bit more. Each day after that, the pig snuffles and snorts his way into the bar during his lunchbreaks. About a week or so after the pig and the barman first began talking, a circus comes to town. The circus owner comes in for a pint at midday one day, just as the pig is ordering a beer. After the initial

shock of seeing a talking pig, the circus owner
approaches him and says, 'Hey, you should
join my circus. You'd make a lot of money.'
'Hang on,' says the pig. 'You work in a
circus right?'
'Yep.'
'That's like one of those tent things, isn't it?
With a big pole in the middle?'
'That's right.'
'The tent's made out of canvas, right?'
'Of course,' replies the circus owner.
'One hundred percent canvas.'
The pig gives the circus owner a very
puzzled look.
'So why in hell would you want a brickie?'

★

A snail crawls into a bar just on closing time. He knocks on the door until the barman finally opens the door, and looks around. When he sees the snail he says, 'Go away. We're closed, and besides, we don't serve snails here.' He then slams the door in the snail's face. The snail again pounds on the door until the bartender gets so frustrated that he opens the door and kicks the snail away. A year later as the bartender is closing up for the night, he hears a pounding on the door again. He opens the door, and who is there but the same snail again. The snail looks up and says, 'What did you do that for?'

A man walks into a psychiatrist's office and says, 'Doctor, I need your help. I think I'm a dog.'
The psychiatrist replies, 'Well get up on the couch and we'll talk about it.'
The guy says, 'Can't. I'm not allowed on the couch.'

LAWS OF LIFE IN MOVIELAND

1. The star detective is always on the brink of retiring when they are handed a case they just *have* to take on.

2. When they are alone, all foreigners speak perfect English to each other.

3. If being chased through town, you can usually take cover in a passing parade, no matter what time of the year it is.

4. It's easy for anyone to land a plane providing there is someone to talk them down.

5. The FBI give their officers personality tests to make sure they are deliberately assigned to a partner who is their exact opposite.

6. All bombs are fitted with electronic timing devices with big red LCD displays so you know exactly when they are going to go off.

7. You will survive any battle in war unless you make the fatal mistake of showing someone a picture of your sweetheart back home.

8. A man will quite happily go fear-free into a fistfight but will always be a big sook when it comes time for his woman to clean his wounds.

9. If anyone hears a strange noise in the middle of the night, it is imperative that they stay and look to see where it's coming from instead of wisely getting the hell out of there.

10. Cars that crash always burst into flames.

11. 'Hello' or 'goodbye' are redundant words when speaking on the phone.

12. The car will never start when a bad guy is chasing you.

13. A detective can solve a case much faster when he has been suspended from duty.

14. Even the most graceful, athletic women always fall down when being chased by a monster or bad guy.

What are the three best things about having Alzheimer's disease?
1. *You can play hide and seek by yourself.*
2. *You can play hide and seek by yourself.*
3. *You can play hide and seek by yourself.*

A man wants a pet that can do anything so he goes to the pet shop and asks the owner if he has any ideas. The shop owner suggests a dog. But the man shakes his head. The owner says, 'How about a cat then?'

The man replies, 'No way! Cats are useless. I want a pet that can do everything!'

The shop owner thinks for a minute, then says, 'I've got it! A centipede!'

The man says, 'A centipede? Hmmm, I've never considered a centipede. Yeah, why not?' So he takes the centipede home.

'Wash the floor,' he tells the centipede and twenty minutes later, the floor is immaculate! He is absolutely amazed.

'Clean the bedroom,' he says next. Twenty minutes later the room is spotless.

The man thinks to himself, 'This is the most amazing thing I've ever seen. This really is a pet that can do everything!' Next he says, 'Run down to the corner and get me a newspaper.'

The centipede walks out the door. Ten minutes later... no centipede. Twenty minutes later... no centipede. Thirty minutes later... still no centipede. The man is wondering what's going on. He can't imagine what could have happened. Did the centipede run away? Did it get run over by a car? Where is that centipede? So he goes to the front door, opens it ... and there's the centipede sitting right outside.

The man says, 'Hey! I sent you down to the corner store half an hour ago to get me a newspaper. What's the matter?'
The centipede says, 'I'm going! I'm going! I'm just putting on my shoes!'

A woman went to her doctor, concerned about the testosterone he had prescribed on her last visit. 'Doc, I think I've been taking too much. I'm growing hair in all sorts of weird places.'
The doctor said, 'That's normal. Testosterone causes hair growth. Just where is it occurring?'
'On my dick.'

A man had been suffering from terrible headaches for years and years. Finally he decided he couldn't stand the pain anymore.

'Doctor, you gotta do something!' he pleaded. 'Well, the latest cure for this type of thing is pretty severe, but we know it works,' replied the doctor gravely. 'It's castration.'

The man was horrified, but could put up with his headaches for no longer. The next week, he underwent the operation. The headaches disappeared as the doctor had promised, and the man landed himself an interview with an important finance company. Needing a new suit for the interview, the man went shopping.

'Looks like you take a size 38,' said the salesman as he pulled some suits off a rack. 'That's pretty good,' said the man. 'How did you know that?'

'Mate, when you've been in this business as long as I have, you get to know this sort of thing.' He then pulled out some underwear. 'Hmm, I guess a 36 for these,' he said. 'Well, you're wrong there,' said the man. 'I've been a 34 for years.'

'No, you're definitely a 36,' insisted the salesman.

'Look, I should know. I always wear 34.'

'Well, okay,' said the salesman. 'But they're going to pinch your balls and give you headaches.'

★

On the top of a tall building in a large city, there was a bar. In this bar, a man was drinking heavily. He would ask the bartender for vodka, then walk out to the balcony and jump off. Minutes later he would be back again and repeat the whole process. This one guy watched this happen a number of times until curiosity got the better of him. Finally he went up to the man and asked, 'Hey, you keep drinking, then jumping off the balcony. And yet, minutes later, you're back up here again, completely fine. How do you do it?'

'Well, that new brand of vodka provides buoyancy so that when I get near the ground, I slow down and land gently. It's fun. You should try it.'

The guy, who was also quite pissed, thought to himself, 'Hey, why not? If he can do it, I guess I can too.' So he went out to the balcony, jumped off, and splat. The guy is dead. The bartender looked over to the other guy and says, 'Superman, you're a real arsehole when you're drunk.'

★

Little Red Riding Hood is skipping merrily home when she sees the Big Bad Wolf crouched down behind a log. 'My, what big eyes you have, Mr Wolf,' says Little Red Riding Hood. The wolf jumps up and runs away! Further down the road Little Red Riding Hood sees the wolf again. This time he is crouched behind a tree stump. 'My, what big ears you have Mr Wolf,' says Little Red Riding Hood. Again the wolf jumps up and runs away. Just near the driveway of her home, Little Red Riding Hood sees the wolf again, this time crouched down behind her letter box. 'My, what big teeth you have Mr Wolf,' taunts Little Red Riding Hood. With that the Big Bad Wolf jumps up and yells furiously, 'Will you f*** off, I'm trying to take a shit!'

★

A guy walks into a bar, carrying three ducks. He puts them down on the bar, and begins chatting with the barman. The barman is experienced and, several hundred jokes later, has learned not to ask people about the animals that they bring into the bar, so he doesn't mention the ducks. After a couple of drinks, the guy goes to the bathroom, leaving the ducks alone with the barman. There is a bit of an awkward silence, so the barman tries to make some conversation.

'What's your name?' He says to the first duck.

'Davey,' says the duck.

'How's your day been?'

'I've been in and out of puddles all day. Had an excellent time.'

'Oh. That's nice,' says the barman. Then he says to the second duck, 'Hi. And what's your name?'

'Dean,' is the answer.

'So how's your day been?'

'Great. Had a ball. Been in and out of puddles all day.'

So the barman turns to the third duck and says 'So, what's your name?'

'My name is Puddles. And don't bother asking about my f***ing day.'

10 THINGS A WOMAN WILL NEVER SAY

1. Don't worry about it. I don't mind you forgetting our anniversary.

2. Are you sure you've had enough to drink?

3. I'm bored. Let's have a threesome!

4. Shouldn't you be down at the pub with your mates?

5. That was a great fart! Do another one!

6. I've decided to stop wearing clothes in the house.

7. You're so sexy with a beer gut.

8. I'd rather watch the footy than go shopping.

9. Let's look at a girlie magazine.

10. Let's tape ourselves in bed tonight and show the guys tomorrow!

Three friends were travelling in the country when their car broke down in the middle of nowhere. After realising that there was nothing they could do to fix it themselves, they decided to walk until they found somewhere to stay for the night. Eventually, after walking several miles, they came across a little house. After knocking for quite a few minutes, a man appeared at the door. The three friends asked if they could stay the night because their car had broken down. 'I'll let you stay here, on one condition,' said the man reluctantly. 'Don't draw any attention to my son. He was born with no ears, and is extremely sensitive about it. I mean it, do not even look at the sides of his head!'

After agreeing to this the three friends were taken into the house and showed the room where they would sleep. The next morning at the breakfast table the son was munching away on toast, and the three friends found they could not help staring at the sides of his head where his ears had been.

'What are you looking at?' demanded the earless boy.

The first of the friends replied, 'I was just admiring your teeth – they are so clean and sharp. Make sure you look after them so you don't ever have to get dentures.'

The second friend said, 'And I was just

admiring your thick head of hair. Make sure you look after it, for you wouldn't want to go bald and have to wear a wig.'

The third said, 'I was just looking at your clear blue eyes. Make sure you take care of them... Lord knows you can't wear glasses.'

A woman got caught in a burning house one day and suffered severe burns to her face. Her husband, sweet man that he was, decided to donate his own skin from his butt so that she could have a skin graft. They agreed to tell no one about where the skin came from, it being rather a delicate matter. After the surgery was completed, everyone was amazed at how well it turned out. The wife looked more beautiful than ever before! (The husband, meanwhile, couldn't sit down for a week.) One day the wife was just so overcome with emotion at her husband's sacrifice she said, 'Darling, you don't know how much I appreciate what you have done for me. There is no way I could ever repay you.' To which he replied, 'My love, think nothing of it. I get thanks enough whenever I see your mother kiss you on the cheek.'

EMPLOYEE TIPS TO MANAGERS

1. If I've done something wrong, tell me first thing Monday morning, as soon as I get in. It's bound to make it a good week for me.

2. If you have an extremely urgent job for me, run in and ask for a progress report every 10 minutes, stressing that you need it done quickly. That helps a lot. Even better, hover behind me as I work – that's sure to produce a good result.

3. Always leave without telling anyone where you are going. It's good for the soul to have a panic attack when an urgent decision has to be made and you're not there to approve it.

4. Never give me work in the morning. Always wait until 4 p.m. and then bring it in to me. The challenge of a deadline is refreshing.

5. Keep me working until 8 p.m. every night. I have no life, no family to go home to. Please realise this and keep me busy every waking second so I don't dwell on it.

6. If I do a job well, don't tell anyone. It'll be our little secret. On the other hand, if I do a terrible job, please bag me to everyone. It's important that we all know our worth in the office environment.

7. If you have special instructions for a job, don't tell me what they are. The best thing is to wait until the job is completed, and then tell me what I should have done. No use confusing me with useful information.

8. Don't give me my annual leave when I want it. Instead, dish it out one day at a time, so I'm not tempted to take an exciting overseas holiday.

9. When you show clients around the building and into our private offices, never bother to introduce me to the people you are with. You and I both know I mean nothing to the company, so don't even glance in my direction as you stand in front of my desk talking with them.

10. Confide in me about your financial woes. I especially like hearing about all the tax you have to pay on that 10K bonus you got at Christmas last year.

★

It was Cam's eighth birthday and he was playing with his new train set on the porch. His mother walked past and heard him say, 'Toot toot! Any f***ing sod who wants to get off the f***ing train better do so now. Any f***ing losers who want to get on, haul your f***ing arses on now!'

Cam's mother was mortified that her son was using such foul language. 'Listen here, young man,' she said sternly. 'We don't use that language in this house. Birthday or not, you go to your room now and stay there for two hours. When you come out, you can play with your new train set, but only if you use nice language.'

Cam sulkily went to his room. Two hours later he came out and began playing with his train set again. Soon the train pulled up at a station and Cam's mother tiptoed out of the kitchen to eavesdop on her son. She heard him say, 'All passengers who are getting off the train, please make sure you leave nothing behind. Thank you for travelling with us today and we hope your trip was a pleasant one.'

She hears her son continue, 'For those of you getting on the train, refreshments will be served in 30 minutes in the dining car. We hope you will have a pleasant and relaxing journey with us today.'

The mother smiled. Then Cam added, 'And for

those of you who are pissed off about the
TWO HOUR delay, go take it out on the f***ing
bitch in the kitchen.'

A health and safety inspector is being shown
the workings of a latex factory by the manager.
The first thing the manager takes him to see is
a machine that makes baby bottle teats.
'Hiss...pop' goes the machine, and the director
explains, 'The hissing sound is caused when
the rubber is injected into the mould. The
popping sound comes from the needle
piercing a hole in the end of the teat.'
The manager then takes the inspector to where
the condoms are being manufactured. The
machine makes a 'hiss, hiss, hiss, hiss-pop'
noise. 'Wait a minute!' says the inspector. 'I
know what the 'hiss, hiss' is, but why does this
machine have a 'pop' sound too?'
'Oh, well, it's just the same as the baby bottle
teat machine,' says the manager. 'It pokes a
hole in every fourth condom.'
'Well, that can't be good for the condoms!'
'Yeah, but it's great for the baby bottle
business!'

Santa is getting ready to take his annual leave, but as usual, more and more problems kept coming up. Four of the elves get food poisioning, the trainee elves start showing their disgruntlement with their low wages by going on a 'work slow' strike, and the toy-producing business falls further and further behind schedule. Then the missus tells him her mother is coming to visit. When Santa goes outside to harness the reindeer he finds that half of them have sauntered off to the waterhole for the afternoon because they don't feel appreciated. More stress. Then, when Santa begins loading the sleigh, one of the boards cracks and his sack of toys falls off, slipping and sliding all across the snow. Frustrated, Santa trudges into the house for a long glass of bourbon. But the elves have hit the liquor cabinet and there is nothing to drink, not even any teenage girly drinks left. In disgust he throws his empty glass down and it explodes into bits all over the floor. Just then the doorbell rings and the cursing, grumbling Santa throws open the door. A little angel is standing on his doorstep, with a great big Christmas tree. And the angel asks ever so sweetly, 'Santa, where would you like me to put this?'

And that, my friend, is how the little angel came to be on top of the Christmas tree...

★

A keen country lad applied for a salesman's job at a city department store. In fact it was the biggest store in the area – you could get anything there. The boss asked him, 'Have you ever been a salesman before?'

'Yes, I was a salesman in the country,' said the lad. The boss thought he'd give the boy a chance and said, 'You can start now. I'll come by at five o'clock and see how you are doing.' The day was long and arduous for the young man, but finally 5 o'clock came around. The boss arrived and asked, 'How many sales did you make today?'

'One,' said the young salesman.

'Only one?' blurted the boss. 'Most of my staff usually make over 30 sales a day. How much was the sale worth?'

'Forty-one thousand, two hundred and sixty-eight dollars,' said the young man.

'How did you manage that?' asked the flabbergasted boss.

'Well,' said the young salesman, 'this man came in and I sold him a small fish hook, then a medium hook and finally a really large hook. Then I sold him a small fishing line, a medium one and a huge one. I asked him where he was going fishing and he said down the coast. I said he would probably need a boat, so I took him down to the boat department and sold him that twenty foot schooner with the twin engines. Then he said his little 1974 Honda Civic probably wouldn't be able to pull it, so I took him to the car department and sold him a new car.'

The boss took two steps back and asked in astonishment, 'You sold all that to a guy who came in for a fish hook?'

'No,' answered the salesman. 'Actually, he came in to buy a box of tampons for his wife and I said to him, "Your weekend's shot, you may as well go fishing."'

A man flew to Las Vegas to gamble, but he lost all his money. All he had left was his plane ticket home, and he had to get to the airport somehow. So he went out to where there was a taxi waiting and explained his situation to the cabby. He promised to send the taxi fare money from home, but to no avail. The cabby said, 'If you don't have fifteen dollars, get the hell out of my cab!'

So the man was forced to hitchhike to the airport and only just made it in time. A few months later the man returned to Las Vegas and this time he won big. Again he went to get a taxi back to the airport. Well who should he see out there, at the end of a long line of taxis, but the cabby who had refused to give him a ride when he was down on his luck. The man